GEORGIA
B&Bs

GEORGIA

B&Bs

Carol & Dan
Thalimer

**Country Roads
Press**

Georgia B&Bs

Published by Country Roads Press
P.O. Box 286, Lower Main Street
Castine, Maine 04421

Cover design by Janet Patterson, Rockland, Maine.
Cover illustration by Dale Swensson based on a photograph
    provided by the Georgia Department of Industry, Trade and Tourism.
Typesetting by Typeworks, Belfast, Maine.

Library of Congress Cataloging-in-Publication Data

Thalimer, Carol.
    Georgia B&Bs / by Carol Thalimer with Dan Thalimer.
        p.   cm.
    Includes index.
    ISBN 1-56626-117-1 : $12.95
    1. Bed and breakfast accommodations—Georgia—Directories.
2. Georgia—Guidebooks.   I. Thalimer, Dan. II. Title. III. Title:
Georgia B and Bs.
    TX907.3.G4T49 1994
    647.9475803—dc20   94-26526
                                                            CIP

Printed in the United States of America.
10 9 8 7 6 5 4 3 2 1

To our parents
for so much

Contents

4. HISTORIC HEARTLAND

5. MAGNOLIA MIDLANDS

6. NORTHEAST MOUNTAINS

7. NORTHWEST MOUNTAINS

8. PLANTATION TRACE

9. PRESIDENTIAL PATHWAYS

Introduction

A bed and breakfast, or B&B, is any home or small nonchain inn that lodges people overnight and includes breakfast. B&Bs fall into various categories. This book uses the categories developed by the Georgia Bed and Breakfast Council.

- Home stay—Less than four rooms in a family home
- B&B inn—Four to thirty rooms set up primarily as a B&B
- B&B hotel/resort—Historic property that operates as a B&B with more than thirty rooms
- Country inn—Primarily a restaurant that also offers rooms for overnight guests

Where a B&B could fit into more than one category, we've placed it in the one we think best describes it.

The recent resurgence of B&Bs started in the seventies when President Jimmy Carter initiated tax incentives for the restoration of historic buildings. Many old derelicts were saved from demolition, but many of their new owners found them too expensive to maintain. Opening them to tourists provided a return on the owners' investment.

Who stays in a B&B? The easiest answer is anyone who likes people and wants some social interaction, a quiet but homey atmosphere, and a personal touch.

Most B&B owners we talk to—especially those in small towns with few quality hotels—indicate that a large portion of their guests are businessmen and -women. The largest growth in B&B patrons is in professional women who have to travel and like the comfort and security of a private home or small inn. Almost anyone who travels alone likes a B&B. In some small towns, a B&B may be the only accommodation.

Another major contingent of B&B guests are people who visit an area to experience it fully. These are the people who truly want to learn about an area— who enjoy meeting people and who are excited by the little differences that make each of us unique.

It is for these types of special travelers that we have written this book.

B&B owners are typically gregarious, openhearted folks who love to meet and get to know all kinds of people. Most are well traveled themselves. Many are older couples whose children have left home, freeing up the rooms for guests, although more and more young people are running B&Bs as a way to help pay the mortgage.

You'll likely be greeted at a B&B with a welcoming cocktail or a cup of coffee and some conversation. Spend a night or two and share a little of your life. We strongly suspect you'll enjoy yourself and may find some new friends. B&Bs have an exceptionally high repeat rate.

In Georgia, about 65 percent of the B&Bs are in private homes. Some are historic houses; others are newly constructed. Most can be found in the mountains of North Georgia or along the historic streets of Savannah, but there are some in every one of Georgia's nine tourist regions. Prices vary from less than $50 to $300; however, 72 percent are less than $75.

DO'S, DON'TS, AND OTHER TIPS

From our visits, a number of commonalities emerged that can assure you a pleasurable visit.

• Make your reservations early, or visit an area that has so many B&Bs, you'll probably be able to find a vacancy. The best places to find large concentrations of B&Bs in Georgia are Savannah, the mountains, and the Presidential Pathways region.

• Never just drop in and expect to get a room. Many B&Bs take guests by reservation only. Because a B&B is often in a person's home, there may be no extra staff. If you aren't expected, the proprietors may not be there.

• Know what you're getting. There's a big difference between the spare room in someone's home and an inn with forty-three rooms spread across six buildings. Properties range from antebellum mansions to primitive farmhouses to brand-new houses. The settings range from downtown locations to isolated mountaintops.

• Many B&Bs don't allow small children, though a few have toys and activities available.

• Many B&Bs don't allow smoking. Those that do often aren't large enough to offer separate areas for smokers and nonsmokers. When a B&B is listed as having restricted smoking, it can mean that smoking is confined to a certain area of the house, but it often means that smoking is allowed only outdoors.

• If a B&B indicates that it has suites, make sure you know what's really being offered. A suite can be anything from a large room with a seating area to a full apartment.

• Many historic houses have a fireplace in every room. However, only a few B&Bs let guests operate the fireplaces.

• Provisions for the disabled vary widely and are often minimal, so check to see exactly what the inn has.

• If you're interested in a specific feature of the property—such as a certain size bed, working fireplace, Jacuzzi, or private deck—be sure to let the proprietor know. Even when a B&Bs lists such amenities, every room doesn't have the same features. Because so many B&Bs are furnished with antiques, king- and queen-size beds can be hard to find.

• Antique furnishings may be elegant, formal, ornate, museum-quality masterpieces or primitive, plain farm pieces. Period reproductions can be fine quality or barely qualify for using the term.

• Few B&Bs have a liquor license and some are in dry counties, so it's best to bring your own alcoholic beverages. However, a few B&Bs prohibit any liquor on the premises (we've indicated those). Most do offer complimentary nonalcoholic beverages.

• Many B&Bs have pets roaming around greeting (or tolerating) the guests, but few allow guests to bring their own. If you're extremely allergic to pets, be sure to check whether the owner has any.

• Discuss how you intend to pay for your stay when you make your reservation. Most B&Bs take major credit cards, but some don't. Clarify which ones are accepted.

• If you intend to stay at a property that has shared baths or where you have to go out in the hall to reach your private bath, remember to bring a bathrobe.

• Many properties are used for other functions, such as luncheons, weddings, receptions, corporate meetings, and so forth. Some have restaurants or shops, so the general public may be wandering through. You can get away from those activities in a large hotel but not in a small establishment. If these types of activities will bother you, it's best to choose a different kind of B&B.

• Breakfast can range from Continental—a roll, juice, and coffee—to a full country breakfast of eggs, choice of meats, grits, a variety of breads, fruits, homemade jams and jellies, quiche, breakfast casseroles, or other specialties. A Continental-plus breakfast may include fresh fruit, a large assortment of breads and pastries, and hot and/or cold cereals. Some B&Bs will try to accommodate your desires or dietary restrictions.

• Most B&Bs serve breakfast buffet style between specified hours, some serve whenever the guest requests, others have one seating. Discuss your desires with the hosts the night before.

• Prices vary considerably, but the average is about $65 to $75.

• Be aware of signage—or the lack thereof. B&Bs that do not accept walk-ins often do not indicate on a sign that they offer lodging. The next problem is where to park, followed by which door to enter. Should you ring the bell or walk in? Lack of signs makes this confusing.

HOW TO USE THIS GUIDE

The Georgia Department of Industry, Trade and Tourism divides the state into nine tourist regions: Atlanta Metro (the city and several surrounding counties), Classic South, Colonial Coast, Historic Heartland, Magnolia Midlands, Northeast Mountains, Northwest Mountains, Plantation Trace, and Presidential Pathways.

We've grouped the B&Bs in this guide in the same way. Each section begins with a description of the region and the major tourist attractions it has to offer. Following in alphabetical order by town or city are the B&Bs in that region. Information about the number of rooms, price, and restrictions are listed at the top of each evaluation, so you'll know whether you want to read further. Unless otherwise noted, credit cards are accepted. Also unless noted, names given under the B&B are the innkeepers, or the owners who are also the innkeepers. At the end of most sections, we've listed several B&Bs that came to our attention just as we were completing the book and didn't have time to inspect.

At the back of the book is a chart categorizing the B&Bs in many ways—a quick reference to the amenities you want in a B&B.

This is the only compendium of bed and breakfasts in Georgia where almost all the B&Bs in the state have been inspected by any person or organization. (Some B&Bs belong to private reservation services and do not wish to be identified in any other manner. Therefore, these are not included and have not been inspected.) Although some other organizations or individuals have inspected B&Bs located in small geographic regions or those belonging to certain organizations, none have inspected them all.

Every B&B reviewed in this guide has been personally visited and evaluated by us; none has paid to be included. However, we have stayed overnight in just a few. Therefore, we can report only our impressions of the physical plant and what the owners tell us about their level of service. Sometimes we interviewed current guests to find out their impressions. We've starred in the index the B&Bs in which we've stayed so you'll know that they got an extra dose of scrutiny.

When studying this book, please keep in mind that, because of the long research time, some of these B&Bs may no longer be in business. Certainly new ones will have opened. Features or policies may have changed. This guide is simply meant to give you some ideas about B&Bs you might want to investigate further.

We've been associated with the travel industry for more than twelve years, during seven of which we owned several travel agencies. For the last six years, we've written about travel for many major publications. Our experience in inspecting hotels and cruise ships includes professional reports for travel agent guides such as *Travel Agent Magazine* and *ABC Star Service*. Because we evaluate B&Bs, we've been asked to speak at several seminars for B&B owners and prospective owners.

OUR RATING SYSTEM

Because every B&B is unique—that's part of their appeal—rating them is like comparing apples and oranges. We didn't want to rate them on purely subjective judgment, so we developed our own rating system. Necessarily it is different from those of such organizations as AAA and Mobil, which rate B&Bs along with hotels and other types of lodgings. Our system applies only to B&Bs.

On a scale of one to five (one being the lowest), we rated both the aesthetic appeal and the condition of the interior, exterior, and grounds. We considered the adequacy of signage and parking facilities. Inside we judged the overall decor and the furnishings as well as whether the B&B offered suites and private and/or shared baths. We evaluated the breakfast as Continental, Continental-plus, full, or gourmet.

We considered such amenities as a TV, VCR, ceiling fan, fresh flowers, cocktails, hors d'oeuvres, afternoon tea, and nightly turn-down service. We looked at such extras as a pool, tennis court, communal Jacuzzi, in-room Jacuzzi, decorative or working fireplaces, gift shop, restaurant, and conference facilities. In addition, we considered how close the B&B is to major tourist attractions. We added up the ratings and divided by the number of features.

To be awarded a rating of five, a B&B needs to be exceptional in many ways, beginning with outstanding architecture and exquisite furnishings. It probably has all private baths, serves a full breakfast, offers numerous amenities, and is close to major attractions. In most cases it features a pool and/or tennis court, one or more Jacuzzis, an in-room working or decorative fireplace, and other special features.

B&Bs with a rating of four offer quite a lot of extras. A rating of three doesn't mean average. It does mean that the B&B is adequate and satisfactory. However, a rating of three probably does have the widest range of differences in quality. Some B&Bs fall in between, so there are some ratings with a half.

Most of the evaluations turned out to be very close to what our subjective judgment was, but a few surprised us. For example, a B&B may more than make up in amenities what it lacks in aesthetic beauty.

Reservation Services and Other Organizations

You can make your own reservations directly with any of the B&Bs listed in this guide. Some reservations can also be made through a reservation service without any additional charge. The advantage of using a reservation service is that you get personal help in choosing the perfect B&B for you. Services also often list B&Bs that do not want to advertise or even be listed as B&Bs in publications.

Georgia Bed & Breakfast is an agency that pairs travelers with more than sixty hosted homes in downtown or suburban Atlanta. Georgia Bed & Breakfast, Reservation Service, 2472 Lauderdale Drive, Atlanta, Georgia 30345. Telephone 404-493-1930.

Bed and Breakfast Atlanta represents 80 to 100 inspected homes in metro Atlanta. Included in the service are a confirmation card, a description of the house, a map of the area, and a map of public transportation. Bed and Breakfast Atlanta, Reservation Service, 1801 Piedmont Avenue, N.E., Suite 208, Atlanta, Georgia 30324. Telephone 404-875-0525 or 800-967-3224.

International Bed & Breakfast Reservations represents a dozen properties in the Atlanta area as well as several throughout the state. International Bed & Breakfast Reservations, 223 Ponce de Leon Avenue, Atlanta, Georgia 30308. Telephone 404-875-9449 or 800-473-9449.

Quail Country Bed & Breakfast coordinates lodging in ten homes in the Thomasville area ranging from modern condos to plantation mansions with private bath and serving Continental breakfast. All accept children. Some accommodations feature a full kitchen. Quail Country Bed & Breakfast Reservation Service, 1104 Old Monticello Road, Thomasville, Georgia 31792. Telephone 912-226-7218.

R.S.V.P. Georgia and Savannah is a free reservation service for B&B inns and guest houses all over Georgia but especially in historic Savannah and along the coast, as well as in Charleston and Beaufort, South Carolina, and Jacksonville and

Saint Augustine, Florida. R.S.V.P. Georgia and Savannah Bed & Breakfast Reservation Service. Telephone 912-232-7787 or 800-729-7787.

R.S.V.P. G.R.I.T.S. (Great Reservations in the South), affiliated with the above entry, represents a select group of inspected and licensed suites, private homes, and guest houses in the Atlanta area. R.S.V.P. G.R.I.T.S, Reservation Service, 541 Londonberry Road, N.W., Atlanta, Georgia 30327. Telephone 404-843-3933. Contact: Marty Barnes.

Savannah Historic Inns & Guest Houses represents eight small inns and private garden suites in restored town houses in Savannah's historic district. These accommodations vary widely in price and personal service. Savannah Historic Inns & Guest Houses, Reservation Service, 147 Bull Street, Savannah, Georgia 31401. Telephone 912-233-7666.

Although the following are not reservation services, they can provide additional information on Georgia bed and breakfasts.

Georgia Bed and Breakfast Council, 600 West Peachtree Street, Suite 1500, Atlanta, Georgia 30308. Telephone 404-873-4482.

Georgia Department of Industry, Trade and Tourism, P.O. Box 1776, Atlanta, Georgia 30301-1776. Telephone 404-656-3590.

1

Atlanta Metro

Atlanta has long been considered the capital of the South. Now the sophisticated city is emerging as a star in the world's firmament. "America's team," the Atlanta Braves, were baseball's National League champions in 1991 and 1992. The metropolis hosted the 1994 Super Bowl. All eyes—internationally—will be on the city when it hosts the 1996 Summer Olympic Games.

We've lived in Atlanta for fifteen years and loved every minute of it. In addition to the city's old-standby attractions, new temptations delight residents and visitors alike.

Stone Mountain—a gigantic granite outcropping northeast of downtown—combines natural scenery with history and modern amusements. We recommend spending a full day there. The park features an antebellum plantation, several museums, a paddle-wheel riverboat, an old-fashioned train ride around the mountain, a petting zoo, a beach, a golf course, and a tramway and hiking trails to the top of the mountain. The main attraction is the towering bas-relief carving on the mountain's escarpment depicting Civil War heroes Robert E. Lee, Stonewall Jackson, and Jefferson Davis. The face of the mountain is also the backdrop for nightly laser shows during the summer. Although the show is different every year, the biggest crowd pleaser is the finale, when the mounted soldiers come to life and circle the mountain.

Underground Atlanta capitalizes on an old system of railroad viaducts and multilevel streets that create a minicity. The complex features a variety of shops, eating establishments, and nightspots. Nearby is **Heritage Row**, a small but excellent museum that traces Atlanta's history from its birth as a railroad terminus. The graceful old depot, located on the plaza, has been restored and contains railroad memorabilia.

Off the plaza is **The World of Coca-Cola Pavilion**, a museum honoring Atlanta's own soft drink. Visitors can taste experimental flavors being considered for the future.

The **State Capitol** is a landmark structure whose dome is covered in Georgia gold. Housed in the Capitol are the **Hall of Flags** and the **State Museum of Science and Industry**.

Other attractions downtown include the **CNN Center**, **Atlanta International Museum**, a branch of the **High Museum of Art**, and **Georgia State University's Art Gallery**. All the downtown attractions are accessible via **MARTA**—the city's rapid rail and bus system.

1

Nearby is the **Martin Luther King, Jr. National Historical Site**. The block-long memorial includes Dr. King's birthplace, Ebenezer Baptist Church, his tomb, and the Center for Nonviolent Social Change. The **APEX Museum** is devoted to African American art and culture.

Other attractions include the **Carter Presidential Library**, with its lavishly landscaped grounds, and **Grant Park**, home of **Zoo Atlanta** and the **Cyclorama**, a circular painting of the Battle of Atlanta.

Visitors will find that Atlanta has several "downtowns." Midtown boasts **SciTrek**, a museum dedicated to science and technology; the recently enlarged **Fernbank Science Center** museum, planetarium, observatory, and IMAX theater; the **Woodruff Center for the Performing Arts**, which contains the **Atlanta Symphony, Alliance Theater, Atlanta Opera**, and the **High Museum of Art**; the **Center for Puppetry Arts**; several other performing arts theaters; **Piedmont Park**; and the **Atlanta Botanical Garden**.

In **Buckhead**, you'll find the **Atlanta History Center** complex, which includes one of the finest Civil War exhibits in the country. The **Governor's Mansion** is nearby. Buckhead is a thriving center for shopping, nightspots, and comedy clubs. One of Atlanta's most enduring summer traditions is the outdoor concert series featuring the Atlanta Symphony Orchestra performing with nationally known artists at **Chastain Park Amphitheater**. Bring your own picnic fare for a preconcert dinner in the park.

Inman Park, the city's oldest suburb, has beautifully restored Victorian homes and a funky commercial district called **Little Five Points**, with shopping, restaurants, theater, and nightlife.

The **West End** is a handsome black neighborhood featuring three historic homes. The **Wren's Nest** was the home of Joel Chandler Harris, who created Uncle Remus.

North of the city you can step back to the early 1880s in Roswell, which boasts fifteen homes that survived the Civil War. The most notable is **Bulloch Hall**—an antebellum Greek Revival mansion—which is open for tours and often hosts period demonstrations. The **Smith Plantation** houses the Roswell Historical Society. The **Roswell Mill**, which produced cloth for Confederate uniforms, now contains shops, restaurants, and nightspots. The **Chattahoochee Nature Center** offers an animal rehabilitation program, nature trails, and a scenic boardwalk.

The **Chattahoochee River** meanders through the metropolitan area, providing swimming, boating, rafting, picnicking, and hiking. Access to the recreational facilities is best in the northwest quadrant.

Marietta has a charming town square surrounded by shops, restaurants, and the popular Theater on the Square.

Ansley Inn

Tim Thomas, Innkeeper
R. Dan York, Owner
253 15th Street
Atlanta, GA 30309
404-872-9000 or 800-446-5416

$95–$250 • Open all year • 33 rooms • B&B
hotel/resort • Kids, call about pets, restricted
smoking, provision for disabled • Rating: 4½

We'd describe the Ansley Inn as among the Ritz-Carltons of B&Bs. In fact, the philosophy of the inn is to offer residential flavor with the service of a first-class hotel. Located in Midtown's elegant and historic Ansley Park neighborhood, this beautifully restored English Tudor mansion offers not only sumptuous accommodations but impeccable service.

The magnificent house has museum-quality paintings, gleaming hardwood and Italian marble floors, massive fireplaces, crystal chandeliers, Oriental rugs, and period pieces from the Chippendale, Queen Anne, and Empire eras. Each guest room has a private bath, phone, wet bar, Jacuzzi, and cable TV. Fresh flowers, champagne, and high-quality bath linens are placed in each room. Many rooms boast decorative fireplaces, and most feature four-poster beds. The accommodations are appealing to business travelers and suitable for small corporate meetings. Weekly, monthly, and corporate rates are available.

A lavish Continental breakfast buffet is served in the public rooms or in your suite. Rates include the buffet, as well as afternoon cocktails, twenty-four-hour concierge service, valet parking, and use of a health club.

The Ansley Inn is near the Woodruff Arts Center, which houses the Alliance Theater, Symphony Hall, and the High Museum of Art. Piedmont Park and the Atlanta Botanical Gardens are also close by, as are four beautiful residential parks.

From I-75/85, exit at Fourteenth Street and go east to Peachtree Street. Turn left and go one block to Fifteenth. Bear right. The inn is just ahead on the right.

Atlanta's Woodruff Bed & Breakfast Inn

Joan and Douglas Jones
223 Ponce de Leon Avenue
Atlanta, GA 30302
404-875-9449 or 800-473-9449 or
FAX 404-875-2882

$65–$125 • Open all year • 12 rooms • B&B
inn • Kids, no pets, restricted smoking
• Rating: 4

We visited this B&B when it was known as Bessie's. Although the inn's name has been changed, Bessie's story is part of what made the establishment so appealing. Starting in the 1950s, she ran a massage parlor frequented by many of Atlanta's movers and shakers. The elaborate board that showed which ladies were occupied remains as a conversation piece.

However, the history of the house started long before Bessie purchased it. It was originally built by Dr. William Orr as a home for his children. The turn-of-the-century Victorian has been faithfully restored with the addition of modern amenities.

Guest rooms are large with high ceilings, and most have private baths. Flexible room arrangements include deluxe suites with private bath, single rooms with private bath, or family suites. Outdoors a gazebo contains a large hot tub.

This B&B is popular with business travelers and is suitable for small corporate meetings. The inn is easily accessible from Downtown and Midtown. Family rates are available.

You may request a Continental or full breakfast, served in the dining room or, at prior request, in your room. In the evening you can relax in the parlor and enjoy Georgia specialties such as peanuts, peaches, and Claxton fruitcake.

Exit I-75/85 at North Avenue and go east. Turn right at Myrtle and go to Ponce de Leon. The inn is on the right at the corner of Myrtle and Ponce de Leon.

Beverly Hills Inn
Mit and Hima Amin
65 Sheridan Drive, N.E.
Atlanta, GA 30305
404-233-8520

$65–$120 • Open all year • 8 rooms • B&B inn
• Kids, pets restricted, restricted smoking
• Rating: 3

Billed as "Atlanta's First Little Inn," the Beverly Hills Inn is an intimate 1929 European-style apartment house in Buckhead that has been converted to a B&B.

Units, all with private bath, have period furnishings and decor—somewhat dated in our opinion. Some rooms have queen-size beds; others have double beds. Rooms are equipped with a phone and TV and each features a private balcony.

Because of the long-term nature of many of the guests, this B&B is more like an apartment building than a hotel. It is suitable for business travelers and small corporate meetings. Corporate relocation and long-term rates are available.

A Continental-plus breakfast of juice, yogurt, coffee cake, French rolls, and fruit is served in the garden room on the lower level.

The staff prides themselves on knowing guests by name. Guests are encouraged to socialize in the first-floor parlor, which offers books, newspapers, and magazines, or in the garden room, which boasts a grand piano. A washer, dryer, and ironing board are available for guests' use.

The inn is conveniently located near public transportation, fifteen minutes from downtown. Shops, restaurants, and entertainment are nearby. An authentic London taxi is available to take you short distances.

Exit I-75/85 at Fourteenth Street. Go east to Peachtree Road—a major north-south thoroughfare through the Buckhead section of Atlanta—and turn left. Sheridan Drive is east of Peachtree at the 2900 block. The inn is on your right.

Heartfield Manor

Sandra Heartfield
182 Elizabeth Street, N.E.
Atlanta, GA 30307
404-523-8633

$40-$60 • Open all year • 1 room, 1 suite
• Home stay • Kids, no pets, smoking,
reservations required, no credit cards
• Rating: 3½

Heartfield Manor is a striking 1903 English Tudor-style cottage in Inman Park—a historic Victorian neighborhood with tree-shaded streets, serene parks, and gracious homes. Architectural features of note in this house include diamond-paned windows, a two-story entrance hall with a grand balcony, stained-glass windows, beamed ceilings, and gleaming wainscoting. The house is furnished with antiques appropriate to the period and style. You'll be fascinated with Sandra's collection of seven fainting couches. Many of the rooms feature fireplaces.

Guest accommodations have private baths. The suite has two rooms, cable TV, phone, microwave, and small refrigerator. It also features a gas fireplace, ceiling fan, and claw-foot tub.

Business travelers, particularly those staying several nights, like the convenience to downtown Atlanta. Corporate and weekly rates are available.

A Continental breakfast is served in your room or the public rooms, or on the front porch or the back deck. Guests are encouraged to use the comfortably furnished back deck and sunporch. Those making long-term stays are welcome to use the washer and dryer.

Heartfield Manor is within walking distance of theaters, restaurants, pubs, shops, and MARTA—Atlanta's rapid rail system. All downtown attractions are easily accessible.

From I-75/85, if you are traveling north, exit at Edgewood Avenue and turn left on Elizabeth Street. If you are traveling south, exit at Butler Street, then turn left onto Edgewood and left onto Elizabeth.

Oakwood House
Judy Hotchkiss
951 Edgewood Avenue, N.E.
Atlanta, GA 30307
404-521-9320

$60–$150 • Open all year • 4 rooms • B&B inn
• Kids, no pets, no smoking, reservations
required • Rating: 4

Named for the huge historic pin oak tree in the backyard, Oakwood House is
located in National Historic Register Inman Park—Atlanta's first suburb—which
was begun in the 1890s. Built in 1911, the post-Victorian house features original
woodwork and exposed brick fireplaces throughout.

Bookshelves fill the walls in the parlor, some bedrooms, and even one
bathroom. The comfortable informal parlor is furnished in natural wicker.

Guest rooms are furnished and arranged for maximum comfort. Judy says,
"I want you to feel like you're staying in a friend's house when she's out of
town." Each room has a private bath, telephone, and comfortable chairs—or in
one case a fainting couch. Beds range from twins to a king. The Master Suite
boasts terry robes and a private deck. Ask about long-term rates.

A Continental breakfast includes healthy baked goods, fresh fruits, juice,
cereal, and hot beverages.

Guests enjoy the front porch with its old-fashioned swing overlooking the
compact perennial garden, or the back decks surveying yet another garden. Lighted
off-street parking is a plus. Word processing and copier service are available, as are
a laundry room and an iron and ironing board. Guests are welcome to use the
refrigerator and microwave. A huge cookie jar in the front hall is always full. Judy
aims to provide "ultimate concierge service." She keeps a large supply of tourist
guides and brochures on hand and is happy to make dining suggestions and
reservations.

From I-75/85, take exit 96, Freedom Parkway. Go east to North Highland
Avenue and turn right. Go to Elizabeth Street and turn left. Go to the second
traffic light and turn right onto Edgewood Avenue. Oakwood House is the fourth
building on the left next door to the historic Trolley Barn.

Shellmont Bed &
Breakfast Lodge
Debbie and Ed McCord
821 Piedmont Avenue, N.E.
Atlanta, GA 30308
404-872-9290

$67–$129 • Open all year • 3 rooms, 1 cottage
• B&B inn • No kids in main house, kids
under 12 in carriage house only, no pets,
restricted smoking, provision for disabled,
reservations required • Rating: 4

A Tiffany stained-glass window and an Adamesque shell festoon and ribbonwork
embellish the facade of this 100-year-old Federalist Greek Revival home that has
been featured in local and national magazines. A City of Atlanta Landmark
Building, it has received the Atlanta Urban Design Commission Award of Excellence and is listed on the National Register of Historic Places.

Twelve-foot ceilings, a built-in velvet settee, ornate plasterwork, and corner
fireplaces accent the antiques, Oriental rugs, and Victorian wall treatments.
Bedrooms have a private bath with an old-fashioned claw-foot tub. There is
handicapped access in the main house by means of an elevator. The cottage suite,
located in the charming back garden carriage house, offers a living room, bedroom, dressing area, and kitchen. Rates are for double occupancy. Additional
guests are $15 extra.

In addition to being pampered, business travelers favor Shellmont because
of its convenient access to downtown and Midtown.

Guests awaken to coffee or tea brought to the second-floor landing. A
Continental-plus breakfast of cereal, dried fruit, fresh fruit, and pastries is served
downstairs using china and linen napkins. Shellmont guests are treated to concierge services, fresh flowers, a basket of fruit, and evening chocolates.

From I-75/85, exit at North Avenue and proceed east to Piedmont Avenue—
a major thoroughfare running north/south from downtown through Midtown.
Shellmont is located at the corner of Sixth Street and is identified by a discreet
sign.

Lilburn Bed & Breakfast

Cheryl and Coleman Walker
901 Cedar Trace
Lilburn, GA 30247
404-923-9813

$50 • Open all year • 1 room • Home stay
• Kids over 5, no pets, no smoking, no credit
cards • Rating: 3

This elegant, recently constructed Georgia-style house is located in an upscale sub-division northeast of Atlanta. The spacious guest room, which has a private bath and a queen-size bed, is furnished in Victorian-era antiques, as is the rest of the house. The guest room also features a private entrance through the garage for those who come in late at night. Children can be accommodated by putting an extra bed in the guest room or by using one of the other bedrooms. Guests can enjoy private use of the formal sitting room with a fireplace and TV, the more informal family room, and the sunroom.

A Continental-plus breakfast including homemade breads is served in the formal dining room or on the sunporch. On request, Cheryl will prepare a full breakfast, which might include grits and a main dish such as French toast or eggs Benedict.

Guests can take advantage of the neighborhood tennis court and swimming pool. Stone Mountain Park is only three miles away, and Atlanta's many attractions are easily accessible.

From I-85 northeast of Atlanta, take the Indian Trail/Lilburn Road exit. Go east six miles. You will have passed through a commercial zone, crossed US 29/State 8, and are proceeding through an area with subdivisions on either side. Look for Cedar Creek Trail on the left. Follow it to the dead end and turn right onto Cedar Trace. The house is the fifth one on the right. It sits on a hill, and part of the front yard has a brick wall around it.

Sixty Polk Street
Bed & Breakfast

Mary and Chet Ladd
60 Polk Street
Marietta, GA 30064
404-419-0101 or 800-497-2075

$75–$85 • Open all year • 4 rooms • Home stay
• Kids over 12, no pets, no smoking, no credit
cards • Rating: 4

Mature trees shade the stately 1872 French Regency Victorian house backed by formal gardens. Inside, twelve-foot ceilings tower over hardwood floors that glow in the light that streams through the floor-to-ceiling windows. Dramatic eclectic furnishings including antiques and reproductions are enhanced by original artworks by Mary's sister.

Guest rooms all feature queen-size beds and private baths (one bath is accessed from the hall). Facilities range from an original claw-foot tub to modern stall showers. The suite has paneled walls and exposed brickwork, a king-size bed, a working fireplace, and a separate wicker-filled sitting room.

Mary describes several menus for the full breakfast she serves in the formal dining room by saying, "If they can eat lunch, I've failed." Weather permitting, guests can eat on the screened porch.

Guests are encouraged to watch TV in the formal living room or curl up with a book in the well-stocked library. The living room, dining room, and library all feature working fireplaces; several of the public and guest rooms have ceiling fans. Guests are welcome to use the refrigerators. Mary provides ice buckets and champagne glasses for guests who bring their own libations.

From I-75 or US 41, take State 120 west one block past the town square. Turn right on Marietta Parkway and go one block; turn left onto Polk Street. The inn is on the corner of Locust and Polk.

The Stanley House
Brigita Rowe
236 Church Street
Marietta, GA 30060
404-426-1881

$75–$85 • Open all year • 4 rooms, 1 suite
• B&B inn • Ask about kids, no pets, restricted
smoking • Rating: 3½

Built in 1895 as the summer cottage of Woodrow Wilson's aunt, this gracious Queen Anne Victorian has a new life as a B&B. The three-story, 5,000-square-foot house is located in Marietta's historic district just a few blocks from the town square. A wraparound porch and a brick-paved courtyard invite guests outdoors.

Thirteen-foot ceilings enhance the formal decor. The sitting room features a working fireplace. A mural embellishes the downstairs hallway. Guest rooms are decorated in antiques and reproductions. Most contain decorative fireplaces and some have queen-size beds. TVs and phones can be provided on request. Private baths feature claw-foot tubs; some have showers. Accommodations in the third-floor suite include a sitting room, loft, refrigerator, skylight, and ceiling fan. Extra guests are an additional $10. The Stanley House is popular with business travelers, those making a long-term stay, and those interested in holding small corporate meetings. Ask about corporate and long-term rates.

A Continental-plus breakfast is served in the formal dining room.

The Marietta town square contains shops, restaurants, and the Theater on the Square, which offers quality live performances throughout the year.

From I-75 northwest of Atlanta, take the Marietta Parkway exit (exit 113). Go west from the exit, which becomes Page Street when you cross US 41. Go about two miles on Page Street, which dead-ends into Church Street. Turn left and go two long blocks. The Stanley House is on the left. Parking is in the rear.

Whitlock Inn

Alexis Edwards
57 Whitlock Avenue
Marietta, GA 30064
404-428-1495

$75–$85 • Open all year • 5 rooms • B&B inn
• Kids over 12, no pets, restricted smoking
• Rating: 4

As the Edwardses explain, "Here in Marietta we hold onto anything that's old: our houses, our furniture, our recipes, and our accents." The Whitlock Inn, a Victorian mansion built in 1900, is a case in point. The restored residence resembles a delicate wedding cake iced with molded panels. The interior is furnished in antiques and reproductions. A floral theme recurs frequently in the wallpapers and fabrics. Each of the five guest rooms has a private bath, working fireplace, queen- or twin-size bed, phone, and ceiling fan. Cable TVs are hidden in antique armoires. Rates are $75 single and $85 double.

An ample Continental breakfast of juice, fruit, breads, and hot beverages is served buffet style in the formal dining room. Afternoon tea is served in the parlor.

In addition to relaxing in a rocker on the wraparound front porch, guests can also enjoy the second-story roof garden or the patio in the shady backyard. Fax and copier service are available.

The Whitlock Inn also serves as a catering facility. A huge ballroom addition can seat more than 100, and smaller rooms are suitable for luncheons, rehearsal dinners, and small business functions.

From I-75 or US 41, take State 120 west past the town square. The inn is the first house on the left in the second block after you pass the square. Parking is in the rear.

Ten-Fifty Canton Street

Andy and Susie Kalifeh
1050 Canton Street
Roswell, GA 30075
404-998-1050

$60–$70 • Open all year • 3 rooms • Home stay
• No kids, no pets, no smoking, no credit cards
• Rating: 3½

The Kalifehs have done such a superb job of renovating a simple late-nineteenth-century cottage in Roswell's historic district that the Roswell Historical Society recently presented them with an Award of Excellence.

The exterior lacks interesting architectural details, but stretching across the front is a large porch equipped with inviting rockers and an old-fashioned swing. Like many cottages, this one is surprisingly large once you get inside. High ceilings enhance the feeling of spaciousness. Guests are welcome to relax in either the formal sitting room or the wicker-filled informal sunroom.

Guest rooms are furnished in antiques. Each has a private bath. One room has a double bed and the other two have queen-size beds. Decorative fireplaces add to the feeling of elegance and romance. Rates are $60 single and $70 double.

The house sits close to a street heavily traveled during the day, but the bedrooms are in the back of the house away from traffic noise. There's plenty of off-street parking both in front of and behind the B&B. Susie operates a beauty salon in an outbuilding.

Breakfast is a Continental-plus meal served in the formal dining room. Snacks can always be found in the butler's pantry just off the kitchen. Cocktails are offered in the afternoon.

Most of historic Roswell is within easy walking distance of this B&B. All of Atlanta's attractions are easily accessible.

From I-285, Atlanta's perimeter highway, take exit 19 to US 19/State 400 north. Take exit 6, Northridge Road. Turn right immediately onto Dunwoody Place and take it until it dead-ends into Roswell Road, where you will turn right. After you cross a bridge, the road changes names to South Atlanta Street. When you come to a Y in the road, take the left fork onto Canton Street. The inn is in the first long block on your left and is well marked by a sign and flags.

2
Classic South

Located in East Central Georgia, the Classic South contains lakes, historical sites, state parks, thriving cities, sleepy small towns, and excellent golf courses.

The area comprises two distinct geographical regions. The fall line—where rivers form falls and rapids—divides the upcountry rolling hills of the Piedmont Plateau from the coastal flatland of the Atlantic Coastal Plain.

Crowning the Classic South region is **Augusta**—Georgia's second oldest city and the largest city in the region. The renowned Master's Golf Tournament is held here annually. **Riverwalk** is a gigantic park along the languid Savannah River. Concerts and other entertainment are held in the amphitheater. Also along Riverwalk are **Port Royal on the Savannah**—a two-level shopping mall—and the **William Moore Art Collection**. The **Cotton Exchange** serves as a welcome center and museum. Old cotton warehouses have been rejuvenated and transformed into boutiques and restaurants. The *Princess Augusta*, a paddle wheeler, makes sightseeing and dinner tours of the river.

Beyond the river, **Sacred Heart Cultural Arts Center**—once a grand Romanesque Revival Catholic church—now serves as the hub for the arts in Augusta. Several other historic buildings are open to the public. Augusta hosts many events, among them the **Augusta Futurity**, the largest cutting horse tournament east of the Mississippi; the **Augusta Invitational Rowing Regatta**; **River Race Augusta**, an outboard motorboat race; and **Hardee's Augusta Southern Nationals**, the world's richest drag boat race.

A driving tour along State 78 follows the route traveled by George Washington in 1791. The town of **Washington**—incorporated in 1780—was the first city in the nation chartered in the name of the president. The **Washington Historical Museum** offers Civil War and Indian relics. Farm life is illustrated at **Callaway Plantation**, a working estate composed of Early American buildings.

In **Crawfordville**, you can tour **Liberty Hall** and a museum featuring Confederate memorabilia. Visit the **Old Market** in Louisville, the state's first capital. **Sandersville** contains the world's largest deposit of kaolin, the white clay used in products as diverse as eye shadow and plastic. While there, visit the **Old Wooden Jail**, where Aaron Burr resided one night. After exploring the subterranean prison cells in **Greensboro's Old Greene County Goal**, enjoy the town's antebellum and Victorian buildings.

Lake Oconee is one of the state's premier lakes and is surrounded by several outstanding golf courses. **Clarks Hill Lake** is noted for its bass fishing. The Classic South region possesses two romantic covered bridges—one in **Watson Mill Bridge State Park** and another in **George L. Smith II State Park**. **Waynesboro** is known as the Bird Dog Capital of the World. The **Georgia Field Trials** is one of the nation's oldest hunting dog competitions.

Oglethorpe Inn

Paula Touchtone
836 Green Street
Augusta, GA 30901
706-724-9774 or 800-241-2407

$85–$125 • Open all year • 18 rooms • B&B
inn • Kids, pets, restricted smoking • Rating: 4

Two adjoining houses and a carriage house contain the eighteen rooms of this elegant red brick Victorian inn. When you enter the foyer you'll be dazzled by the beautiful stained-glass window and intricate carving on the staircase.

Each guest room is decorated with period reproductions. All rooms offer private baths and some feature Jacuzzis. Some rooms have king- or queen-size beds.

Oglethorpe Inn is popular with business travelers. The public rooms of the second house are often used for private parties such as bridal luncheons and wedding receptions. These rooms are also suitable for small corporate meetings.

A full country breakfast is served in the dining room, or you can request breakfast in bed.

Flowers and wine will make you feel welcome. Your bed will be turned down nightly and a treat left on your pillow. Pamper yourself in the pool or the courtyard hot tub.

The inn is accessible to Augusta's many attractions, and water sports abound on the river and at nearby Clarks Hill Lake.

From I-20, take exit 65, which is Washington Road. As you enter downtown Augusta, it becomes Broad Street. Turn right onto Ninth, then left onto Greene. The inn is on the right.

Partridge Inn

Joel Sobel
2110 Walton Way
Augusta, GA 30904
706-737-8888 or 800-476-6888

$75–$125 • Open all year • 105 suites
• Country inn • Kids, no pets, restricted
smoking, provision for disabled • Rating: 5

Augusta can be justly proud that the Partridge Inn is one of only two historic Georgia inns chosen as members of the National Trust for Historic Preservation's Historic Hotels of America.

What began as a private residence in 1879 was enlarged until it became one of the country's first all-suite inns. Faithfully restored and graciously furnished, the five-story, 105-suite inn boasts a quarter mile of porches and private balconies. You can hardly imagine anything more southern than relaxing on one of these verandas with a cool drink.

The sizes of the suites vary from an efficiency to a several-room apartment. Most suites offer a full kitchen, sitting room/dining area, bedroom, and private bath. Furnishings and fabrics are tasteful period reproductions. A few suites feature a private veranda. The inn has a swimming pool, parking deck, and complimentary valet parking.

Partridge Inn is favored by business travelers and is particularly suitable for corporate meetings.

A complimentary light breakfast buffet is served each morning in the informal cocktail lounge, or it can be taken onto the expansive second-floor balcony. Lunch and dinner are offered in the formal, plantation-style dining room. Cocktails and hors d'oeuvres are available from late afternoon into the evening.

From I-20, take exit 65 onto Washington Road. Turn right onto Berckman Road. Bear left onto Highland, then turn left onto Walton Way. The inn is on the right soon after you pass Augusta College.

The Davis House

Terri Long, Innkeeper
Norman Zapien, Owner
106 North Laurel
Greensboro, GA 30605
706-453-4213

$75-$90 • Open all year • 7 rooms • B&B inn
• Kids over 12, no pets, no smoking • Rating: 4

Owner Norman Zapien is a well-known hair stylist in Atlanta. Purchasing, restoring, and opening The Davis House as a B&B has fulfilled one of his dreams. Norman works in his salon Monday through Thursday and spends Friday through Sunday in Greensboro. This is the only B&B we know of where guests can make arrangements for such in-house spa services as manicures, pedicures, massages, facials, and haircuts and -styling.

The stately red brick mansion sits well back from the street hidden behind a dense stand of ancient magnolias. The sweeping circular drive deposits you at the front entrance and many expansive porches. Step through the vestibule into a foyer big enough to be a ballroom. Fourteen-foot ceilings soar over gleaming wood floors, decorative fireplaces, and family antiques. In addition to the formal dining room and music room, the downstairs has an informal enclosed sunporch furnished with rattan and offering a TV. Guest rooms feature fresh flowers and fleecy bathrobes. Some rooms are air conditioned and some offer working fireplaces. One room has a private porch. Some baths feature claw-foot tubs. The Davis House is appropriate for business travelers and ideal for small corporate retreats.

Guests can enjoy a breakfast of their choice in the formal dining room or the kitchen, or on the porch or by the pool. Shelves in both the pantry and the refrigerator are set aside for guest use.

The Davis House offers a swimming pool, tennis courts, lawn games, and even horses. Nearby Lake Oconee has fishing, waterskiing, and sailing. Golf is available at Reynolds Plantation and Harbor Club.

From I-20, take exit 53 north onto State 44. Go three miles into town and turn left at the traffic light. Go three blocks and turn right onto North Laurel. The inn is the second house on the left.

Early Hill

Kevin Shockley
1580 Lickskillet Road
Greensboro, GA 30648
706-453-7876 or 404-873-2822

$50–$70 • Open all year • 5 rooms • B&B inn
• Kids, no pets, no smoking • Rating: 3

Built around 1820, this lovely Georgian farmhouse was the centerpiece of an 11,000-acre cotton plantation. Now it sits on parklike country grounds totaling 25 acres of peace, quiet, and tranquil views. You can enjoy the surroundings from the porch or take long walks on the grounds.

Inside, the decor is surprisingly formal. From the central hall, an unusual "flying" staircase rises to the second floor. The formal parlor contains a grand piano. More casual is the "easy" room, which features a TV and a woodstove.

The bedroom decor and bedding arrangements vary, but all guest rooms have ceiling fans and armoires. Two bedrooms offer twin beds and share a bath. The king and double rooms have private baths. The attic room can sleep four with its two twins and a daybed with a trundle.

Because of the inn's isolation, we were surprised to learn that it is popular with business travelers. It would also be suitable for family reunions and small corporate meetings. Corporate and group rates are available.

A full breakfast of sausage, grits, biscuits, and toast is served.

The inn sports a regulation croquet lawn. Guest privileges are offered at Lake Oconee, with its fishing, golf, tennis, and horseback riding. Deer and turkey hunting are popular.

From I-20, take exit 53 and turn north on State 44. Go 1.5 miles beyond Greensboro, then turn left on Lickskillet Road. The inn is on the right.

Into the Woods
Gwen Risser, Innkeeper
Robert Risser, Owner
Greiner Road
Hephzibah, GA 30815
706-554-1400 or 717-762-8525

$45–$85 • Open spring to fall • 4 rooms
• B&B inn • Kids, no pets, no smoking
• Rating: 3

Located just a few miles south of Augusta, this B&B leaves the city behind for a restful wooded oasis. The house was built in the 1800s in Waynesboro, then moved to its present location and completely refurbished. High-ceilinged rooms are furnished in Victorian antiques, all of which are for sale. Guests are encouraged to enjoy the working fireplace in the living room and the cozy wicker furniture on the porches.

Guest rooms feature queen-size beds and fresh flowers. One room offers a private bath; the other three share one and a half baths. Several rooms have ceiling fans. One bedroom features an extra daybed, and the inn can supply an antique crib.

The woodsy country setting makes this B&B ideal for family reunions. Miles of country lanes entice visitors to take long, peaceful walks.

Guests can enjoy their full breakfast in the formal dining room or informal breakfast nook, or on the back porch. The southern-style meal might include grits, biscuits, a casserole, homemade breads, jams, and jellies.

Augusta's Riverwalk and variety of restaurants are only minutes away.

From US 25 traveling south from Augusta, turn west on Greiner Road eight miles south of the junction of State 88. Follow the signs to the inn on Longhorn Road.

Coleman House

Ron and Karen Horvath
323 North Main Street
Swainsboro, GA 30401
912-237-2822

$55–$85 • Open all year • 10 rooms • B&B inn
• Kids, no pets, restricted smoking • Rating: 4

Built between 1901 and 1904, this majestic three-story Victorian mansion is painted in the traditional manner of the style—a predominant color with several trim colors. In this case, the predominant color is cream and the trim consists of subdued rust, blue, and brown. The house sits well back from the street on a three-acre lot.

The Horvaths have done such a magnificent job of restoring the thirty-two-room house—listed on the National Register of Historic Places—that they received an award from the Georgia Trust for Historic Preservation.

Inside you'll find twelve-foot ceilings, intricate molding, Bradbury & Bradbury wallpaper, and eleven fireplaces. This is one of only three surviving houses in Georgia with burl-pine floors. The central hall of this 10,000-square-foot mansion is fifty-five feet long and is often the scene of weddings and other functions. There's a wraparound porch on the main level and several upstairs porches. Polygonal gazebo-like turrets complete with conical roofs and finials accent the veranda corners.

All ten guest rooms feature private baths with claw-foot tubs, decorative fireplaces, and period antiques. Most have double beds, but several have twins. Rooms offer cable TV, ceiling fans, and phones. This inn is appropriate for business travelers and is particularly well suited for small corporate meetings. Long-term and corporate rates are available. Additional guests in the same room are $10 extra.

A full breakfast is served in the dining room, or on the porch if weather permits.

Fishing, golf, and tennis are available nearby.

From I-16, take exit 21 and turn north on US 1. Go approximately fourteen miles to Swainsboro, continue across US 80, and stay on US 1 for two and a half blocks. The inn is on the right.

Edenfield House Inn

Imogene and Jim Buckley
358 Church Street
Swainsboro, GA 30401
912-237-3007

$45-$55 • Open all year • 9 rooms • B&B inn
• Kids, no pets, restricted smoking • Rating: 4

All innkeepers profess to offer a personal touch; however, few have trained, as Imogene Buckley has, at the Ritz-Carlton—renowned for its impeccable service.

This beautifully restored 1895 home is located in a historic neighborhood on a well groomed lot dotted with dogwoods and huge pines and oaks. In fact, Edenfield House has won a beautification award from the city.

The handsomely carved front door is surrounded by beveled glass and opens into a spacious foyer, decorated with seven beautifully hand-painted murals. Other exquisite details include original wood moldings and gilded mirrors. The house is furnished in antiques and period reproductions. A parlor brimming with art objects from around the world, an airy sunroom, and a wraparound porch invite guests to read or just spend quiet time.

Each high-ceilinged guest room features a private bath, TV, and phone. Bed sizes vary. Rollaway beds are available. A few rooms have four-poster beds, decorative fireplaces, and ceiling fans. Ask about family rates. Edenfield House is popular with business travelers and is suitable for small business meetings.

A Continental breakfast, served on Royal Doulton china with French crystal, Towle silver, linen tablecloths, and fresh flowers, is offered in the dining room with a complimentary morning newspaper. Guests can choose items from the menu at an additional cost.

The inn is conveniently located for sight-seeing in Macon, Milledgeville, Augusta, and Savannah.

From I-16, take exit 19 onto State 56. After entering the city limits, turn left at the second caution light. Go three blocks. The inn is on the right.

1810 West Inn
Gina White
254 North Seymour Drive, N.W.
Thomson, GA 30824
706-595-3156

$45-$55 • Open all year • 8 rooms • B&B inn
• Kids over 12, no pets, restricted smoking
• Rating: 3½

This typical Piedmont Plains farmhouse was built in 1810 entirely of heart pine with unique detailed molding. Five attached buildings create a rambling structure. An additional cottage was built in 1900. Although the sweeping drive, lavish lawns, shade trees, and garden on more than ten acres make the setting appear to be in the country, the inn is conveniently located near the city and I-20. Because of its location, the 1810 West Inn attracts both corporate and leisure travelers.

The house was built by the Butler West family, in whose possession it remains. Large porches—some screened—with ceiling fans allow guests to enjoy the serenity of the big yard and garden. The guest rooms are named after family members or illustrious citizens. Many rooms have decorative fireplaces—six work. Although the house is air conditioned, some rooms also feature ceiling fans. Beds are twins, doubles, and a few queens. Two rooms feature private porches with comfortable chairs. The cottage has four bedrooms—a twin, two queens, and a double—as well as four private baths. Rates are for double occupancy; additional guests in the same room are $10 extra. The inn is suitable for business travelers and small corporate meetings. Corporate and group rates are available. Country club privileges are available to guests who want to play tennis or golf.

An especially ample Continental-plus breakfast is served at the huge dining room table. Wine, fruit, and cheese are served at cocktail time.

From I-20, take exit 59 south.

Four Chimneys Bed and Breakfast

Ralph and Maggie Zieger
2316 Wire Road
Thomson, GA 30824
706-597-0220

$35–$50 • Open all year • 4 rooms • Home stay
• Ask about kids, no pets, smoking • Rating: 3½

Manicured lawns and color-splashed gardens surround the 1820s farmhouse, but the first things you'll notice are the massive chimneys. The retention of original hand-planed heart pine floors, walls, and ceilings—sometimes painted and stenciled—enhance the formal country decor, as do the antiques.

Guest rooms feature working fireplaces and four-poster or canopy queen-size beds. Two rooms have private baths. The two rooms that share a bath down the hall are usually used for a family or friends traveling together, so in essence you'll have a private bath.

Guests enjoy the wicker furniture, the old-fashioned swing on the wide front porch, and the well-tended herb garden.

A generous Continental-plus breakfast is served in the formal dining room. Breakfast might include croissants, bagels, English muffins, homemade scones or muffins, dry cereal, fresh fruits and juices, and hot beverages.

The hospitable Ziegers offer their guests coffee, tea, or iced tea on arrival. Sherry or port are available, as are books, a TV, and board games. Outdoor types will enjoy the state parks, golf, and fishing nearby.

Room rates are $35–$40 single and $45–$50 double, with the exception of Masters Golf Tournament week in early April when special rates are in effect.

From I-20, take State 17 south all the way through town. Go 3.5 miles from the railroad tracks and depot, and at a large church on the left, turn left onto Wire Road. The imposing gray house with four chimneys is 1.2 miles on the right; the name is on the mailbox.

Blackmon Bed and Breakfast
Eleanor and Steve Blackmon
512 North Alexander Avenue
Washington, GA 30673
706-678-2278

$45 • Open all year • 2 rooms • Home stay
• Kids, no pets, restricted smoking, no credit
cards • Rating: 3½

Wingfield is the actual name of this exquisitely restored and remodeled 1786 farm-house owned by the Blackmon family. Accommodations are in a fully equipped apartment on the garden level, overlooking a beautifully landscaped yard. The cozy guest quarters feature brick and paneled walls as well as a fireplace with a woodstove insert. The bookcases flanking the fireplace are well stocked. A sofa and comfortable chairs form a conversation area around the fireplace. Other amenities include a TV, a VCR, an exercise bike, and a small kitchen. A crib can be provided. The rate is $45 per couple. Each extra person is an additional $5.

A Continental-plus breakfast is served in the dining room or on the back porch. Breakfast may include hotcakes, cereal, fruit, homemade breads, jellies, and jams. You'll be welcomed with wine and a fruit and cheese tray.

From I-20, take exit 55 onto State 47 north to US 78. Turn right. At the fourth traffic light, turn left onto North Alexander Avenue. The inn is on the left.

Holly Ridge Country Inn

Vivien and Roger Walker
2221 Sandtown Road
Washington, GA 30673
706-285-2594

$49–$65 • Open all year • 10 rooms • B&B inn
• Kids, no pets, restricted smoking, provision
for disabled, no credit cards • Rating: 3½

One of the most unusual B&Bs we've discovered is the Holly Ridge Country Inn, located on 100 acres near Washington. The brainchild of Vivien and Roger Walker, the inn is actually two completely dissimilar houses that Vivien wanted to save from the wrecking ball. Not only did she save and refurbish them, but she moved them to her property. Fronting the country road is a stately red Victorian house with quaint towers and generous porches. Behind this house and attached to it at right angles is an ancient farmhouse once lived in by Vivien's great-grandparents.

The ambience in each house is entirely different, so be sure to state your preference for formal or informal. The interior decor and furnishings of the Victorian house are formal, befitting the exterior; the interior of the farmhouse is rustic, and its furniture is unadorned country style. The newer house has a wraparound porch with lots of wicker and swings. The older house has a small porch with rockers. Both houses are air conditioned and have ceiling fans. The guest rooms in both houses are unique in color scheme and furnishings.

The Victorian house features high ceilings, beautiful moldings, a huge central hall, a parlor, and a dining room that will seat forty-five people and is often the scene of weddings, receptions, luncheons, showers, and parties. A large upstairs hall can serve as a sitting room for guests if a major activity is in progress downstairs. The older, more rustic house has floors, walls, and ceilings of exposed heart-pine boards.

Breakfast—either Continental or a full meal—is generally served in the sunroom of the Victorian house, or on one of the expansive porches in good weather.

The grounds include a pond, plenty of lawn furniture, and trails for biking and hiking. Those who want to roam can explore the barn and the remains of an old country store. Sports lovers can enjoy nearby fishing, golf, and turkey and deer hunting.

From State 44 east of Washington, go eight miles to Sandtown Road and turn right. The inn is one-half mile ahead on the left.

Georgia's Guest Bed & Breakfast
Georgia Carroll
640 East 7th Street
Waynesboro, GA 30830
706-554-4863

$40–$57 • Open all year • 3 rooms, 1 suite •
Home stay • Kids over 12, no pets, no smoking,
reservations preferred • Rating: 3

This two-story Georgian-style home built in 1926 was once the centerpiece of a 650-acre dairy farm on the outskirts of Waynesboro. Now most of the land has been sold for commercial or residential use. However, the house maintains its stately dignity at the head of a sweeping circular driveway.

Beveled-glass doorways, gleaming oak or heart-pine flooring, and ornately carved mantels are a few of the features. Guests are encouraged to use the large formal sitting room. Guest rooms have period antiques and an eclectic assortment of newer pieces. The suite, located on the ground floor, features a bedroom, private bath, and sunroom with a fireplace, TV, and desk. Upstairs, two rooms share a bath; the other has a private bath. Inquire about family rates. The inn welcomes business travelers.

A Continental or full breakfast is served in the sunny formal dining room. Georgia is an exceptional hostess. She knows how to make her guests feel at home immediately. As soon as you arrive, she'll serve you cold spiced tea or hot spiced cider, depending on the weather, then remain handy to serve you.

Good fishing, golf, and tennis are available nearby. Visit the nearby Burke County Museum. Occupying a restored antebellum home, it displays the early history of the county as well as the history of cotton.

The inn is located on the right side of State 56 south, 0.7 mile from the Waynesboro Courthouse.

NEWLY OPENED

The Belle Sterling B&B
Barbara Homen
412 East Robert Toombs Avenue
Washington, GA 30673
706-678-5388

3

Colonial Coast

Georgia's Colonial Coast region offers traditional southern hospitality in a scenic historical setting. The region boasts Savannah, the Golden Isles, several historically significant coastal towns, and the Okefenokee Swamp.

Savannah is the crown jewel of the region. Most tourists come here for a walk through history in the nation's largest historic district—2.2 square miles of vigorously and lovingly restored buildings on the National Register of Historic Places, twenty-one restful squares, house/museums, shops, restaurants, and more than twenty bed and breakfasts. The **Savannah Visitor Center**, located in an old railroad depot just off Montgomery Street, has two audio-visual presentations and exhibits that will orient you.

Riverfront Plaza, a nine-block esplanade dotted with fountains, benches, and plantings, makes an ideal place to observe the busy Savannah River or just people watch. Many festivals throughout the year are centered at the plaza. The **Ships of the Sea Museum** traces Savannah's important shipbuilding and maritime history. **Emmet Park**, shaded by live oaks and dripping with wisps of Spanish moss, contains several memorials to Savannah's history. The **City Market** is two restored blocks that contain restaurants, nightspots, and shops. You'll want to explore Savannah's house/museums, churches, and fascinating cemeteries. **Forsyth Park** has tennis and basketball courts, a playground, jogging and walking trails, and a fragrance garden for the blind.

Other museums in Savannah include the **Central of Georgia Railroad Roundhouse Complex**, the **Savannah History Museum**, the **Savannah Science Museum**, the **Telfair Academy of Arts and Sciences**, and the **Beach Institute African-American Cultural Center**.

You can tour the city in a horse-drawn carriage or cruise on the paddle wheelers *Spirit of Savannah* and *Savannah River Queen*.

When you're hungry we recommend the famed **Mrs. Wilkes Boarding House**, which the Condé Nast *Traveler* rates as one of the top fifty restaurants in the nation. It serves southern home cooking family style for breakfast and lunch.

Not far from Savannah are **Old Fort Jackson**, **Fort Pulaski National Monument**, **Skidaway Island State Park**, **Skidaway Marine Science Complex**, the shrimping village of **Thunderbolt**, and **Wormsloe Historic Site**.

Tybee Island, which begins the chain of Georgia's thirteen barrier islands, offers five miles of white sand beaches on the Atlantic just fifteen minutes east of

Savannah. The town retains its 1950s ambience. Attractions include **Fort Screven**, the **lighthouse and museum**, the **Marine Science Center**, a water slide, an amusement park, and charter fishing boats.

At **Richmond Hill**, you can explore key earthwork fortifications used to defend Savannah during the Civil War. In tiny **Midway**, a church built by the Puritans in 1792 still stands.

Darien—Georgia's second oldest town—boasts historic squares, a district of timber barons' homes, sea captains' residences, a shrimp fleet, and caviar processing. The Blessing of the Fleet is a spring tradition. At **Fort King George Historic Site**, the authentically costumed staff demonstrates life at a Revolutionary War fort. From Darien, you can take a boat ride to **Sapelo Island**—a naturalist's paradise.

Brunswick—the Shrimp Capital of the World—is the gateway to the **Golden Isles** but has charms of its own. **Old Town Brunswick**, laid out in 1771, retains thirty-six significant architectural sites. Other attractions include the **shrimp docks, "Liberty Ship" model, Mary Miller Doll Museum**, and several **wildlife management areas**. Nearby is the **Hofwyl-Broadfield Plantation**, a working antebellum rice plantation where you can see a movie, take a walking tour, and visit the museum.

The **Golden Isles** include St. Simons, Little St. Simons, Sea, Cumberland, and Jekyll Islands. On **St. Simons** explore **Fort Frederica** and the **Lighthouse & Coastal Museum**. St. Simons offers fabulous golf as well as other sports. **Little St. Simons** is one of our favorite places. Privately owned, this unspoiled 10,000-acre barrier island offers guest accommodations in spring and fall. A limited number of people can make a day trip to the island. State-owned **Jekyll Island** was the exclusive getaway of millionaires such as the Rockefellers, Vanderbilts, Pulitzers, Astors, and Morgans. Their "cottages" have been restored and are open for public tours. **Cumberland Island**—a wild, pristine national park—is accessible by ferry. In addition to campers and the guests of Greyfield Inn, only 300 day-trippers are allowed. Ruins remain of several millionaires' estates, but most people come for the island's natural beauty.

The charming fishing village of **Saint Marys** has thirty-eight historic sites, including a description in Braille. The Toonerville Trolley of comic strip fame resides along the main street. The **McIntosh Sugar Mill Tabby Ruins** are the largest and best-preserved tabby structures on the coast. Tabby—a building material made of oyster shells, sand, and water—is unique to the Georgia coast. The new Osprey Cove golf course offers seventy-two holes overlooking the marshes.

Inland is the "land of the trembling earth"—the Okefenokee Swamp—a labyrinth of marshes and rivers that is home to a large variety of wildlife. Canoe tour guides will enchant you with swamp tales while pointing out alligators, flora, and fauna. The swamp has a network of boardwalks and observation towers as well as an interpretive center.

Brunswick Manor/
Major Downing House
1890 House

Claudia and Harry Tzucanow
825 Egmont Street
Brunswick, GA 31520
912-265-6889

$45–$100 • Open all year • 5 rooms, 2 grand
suites, 2 cottages • B&B inn • Ask about kids
and pets, no smoking, provision for disabled,
no credit cards • Rating: 4

Together, the stately brick Major Downing House, built in 1886, and the simpler
frame house next door, built in 1890, serve as a B&B facing Halifax Square in
historic Old Town Brunswick. Between the two houses are a greenhouse, garden,
fish pond, and fountain.

The manor house is furnished with antiques and reproductions. The original carved oak staircase rises grandly to the second floor, and deep stained-glass
"eyebrow" windows afford lovely views.

Each guest room is decorated in turn-of-the-century style. The rooms in the
manor are more formal and have private baths; those in the 1890 House are more
casual and share a bath. Rooms are equipped with king- or queen-size beds, TV,
and VCR. Some feature decorative fireplaces and/or kitchenettes. Each room is
supplied with fresh flowers, fruit, sherry, luxuriant terry bathrobes, and designer
linens. Corporate rates are available. Inquire about long-term rates.

A full gourmet breakfast featuring local specialties is served in the formal
dining room. Enjoy afternoon high tea in the garden or on the porch.

Harry is a train buff. He'd love to tell you about his collection. The
Tzucanows have many vintage automobiles, including several Jaguars. If you're
flying in, arrange to be picked up at the airport in one of them. In addition, Harry
and Claudia have two large boats and operate fishing charters. Fishing and golf
are available nearby.

From I-95, take exit 7 and the ramp south—US 341 to Brunswick. Go about
seven miles on US 341, which turns left on Prince Street. Stay on Prince for four
major blocks to Egmont Street. The inn is on the corner of Prince and Egmont.

Rose Manor Guest House and Tea Room

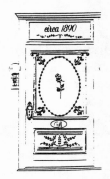

Rachel Rose
1108 Richmond Street
Brunswick, GA 31520
912-267-6369

$45–$95 • Open all year • 4 rooms • B&B inn
• Kids, no pets, restricted smoking, no credit
cards • Rating: 3½

Located on Hanover Square in historic Old Town Brunswick, this 1890 Victorian bungalow has been faithfully restored and graciously furnished with antiques. Typical of Victorian houses, Rose Manor has a wicker-filled wraparound porch. Adding a whimsical look to the entrance is an elegantly carved front door with a rose etched into its oval glass. The cottage is surrounded by English formal gardens displaying many roses.

Each guest room has a decorative fireplace, elegant antiques, and a floral motif. Floating cable and phone hookups are available. The four guest rooms are served by three baths with claw-foot tubs and old-fashioned showers. Family rates are available. The inn is appropriate for business travelers and small corporate meetings.

A gourmet Continental-plus breakfast is served in the formal dining room, the wraparound porch, the garden, or in bed. High tea is served in the afternoon. A small refrigerator can be supplied to each guest room if requested. Rachel has put together several luxury packages appropriate for honeymoons, anniversaries, or other special occasions. For an additional fee she will include a candlelight dinner, champagne, a cheese tray, and breakfast in bed. The tearoom is available for parties by reservation.

From I-95, take exit 7 and go east on US 341. Turn left at Newcastle Street and proceed straight through the commercial district to Hanover Square. Rose Manor is on the left side of the square.

Greyfield Inn
Mary Jo Ferguson
8 North Second Street
Fernandina Beach, FL 32035-0900
904-261-6408

$275-$315 • Open all year • 11 rooms • B&B
hotel • Kids over 6, no pets, restricted smoking
• Rating: 4½

Although the mailing address of this inn is in Florida, the inn is, indeed, in Georgia. In fact, it is the only accommodation on Cumberland Island, the largest and southernmost of the state's barrier islands and also a national seashore operated by the National Park Service.

A stay at Greyfield is a true getaway. There are only a few private residences on the island, and only a few private and park service vehicles are permitted. Access to Greyfield is only via a private ferry from Fernandina Beach.

At the turn of the century, the island was privately owned by the Carnegie family. In the 1960s, Greyfield opened as an inn. Today all the property except Greyfield has been donated to the National Park Foundation.

Greyfield sits on 1,300 private acres within an easy walk of the beach. It is furnished just as it was in 1901. Some rooms share a bath. An expansive front porch furnished with rockers and large swings is a favorite retreat.

Three gourmet meals per day are included: a hearty full southern breakfast, picnic lunch, and a formal dinner (jackets are suggested for gentlemen).

There are ceiling fans in each room. During the winter months fires are kept burning in the living room and dining room. A well-stocked bar operated on the honor system is maintained in the old gun room. Hors d'oeuvres are served in the bar each evening. Bicycles are available to rent. There are no stores on Cumberland Island, so bring everything you think you'll need. In winter, bring hats, gloves, scarves, and a warm jacket or windbreaker.

The island offers twenty miles of pristine beaches and miles of hiking trails. Visitors, including campers and day-trippers, are strictly limited to 300 per day. Instead of swarms of tourists, visitors are likely to see wild horses, deer, armadillos, and numerous species of birds. A small museum contains memorabilia tracing the island's history, and you can explore around the ruins of Dungeness and Stafford mansions.

Call (8 A.M. to 5 P.M. Monday to Friday) for reservations and instructions for meeting the ferry.

Open Gates

Carolyn Hodges
Vernon Square
Darien, GA 31305
912-437-6985

$48–$61 • Open all year • 4 rooms • Home stay
• Kids over 8, no pets, no smoking, no credit
cards • Rating: 3½

Built in 1876, this 116-year-old house is filled with period furniture and family collections. Carolyn is an artist and a musician. Several years ago one of her paintings was selected by Atlanta's "Save the Fox" campaign, printed as a poster, and
sold to raise the money necessary to preserve and restore the town's grand theater.
The original painting hangs in the formal parlor. Also in the parlor are a grand
piano, violin, and trumpet. Carolyn might be persuaded to play for you.

The cozy library offers a view of the sweeping lawns as well as comfortable
furniture, a fireplace, a TV, books, games, puzzles, and maps. Two guest rooms
have private baths and two share a bath. Bedding configurations vary, with
several king- and queen-size beds. Rates are for double occupancy; additional
guests in the same room are $10 extra. Guests are welcome to use the swimming
pool, Jacuzzi, and brick barbecue or to relax in the comfy hammock. Flowers in
your room add to the ambience of welcome.

A Continental-plus breakfast is served in the formal dining room with
china, silver, crystal,and even name cards. Carol collects unusual jam pots, which
are filled with homemade preserves.

From I-95, take either exit 9 or 10 onto US 17. Turn east at Monroe and
proceed to Vernon Square. The inn is identified by a sign.

Blueberry Hill
Rachel Lyons
Route 1, Box 253
Hoboken, GA 31542
912-458-2605

$50 • Open all year • 2 cottages • Country
inn • Kids, no pets, provision for disabled
• Rating: 3

Blueberry Hill is about as off the beaten track as you can get. The unique property consists of a Cajun restaurant—housed in a 123-year-old log cabin—and two cottages on fourteen wooded acres. The property is located in an isolated country setting reached by several dirt roads. However, the signage is good so it's easy to find.

Rachel Lyons learned hotel management as an executive with Howard Johnson's and the restaurant business as part of the Morrison's Cafeteria chain. She learned her Cajun cooking skills while living in the bayous of Louisiana.

Two rustic cottages are tucked away among the oak trees, azaleas, dogwoods, redbuds, and wild blueberry bushes. The cottages, which have one bedroom and one bathroom each, are furnished with mismatched semiantique furniture and have no phone, TV, or radio. One cottage has a double bed; the other has a double and a twin.

A full breakfast is served on the enclosed porch of the restaurant. Appropriately, you have a choice of blueberry hotcakes and bacon or blueberry muffins, bacon, and eggs.

Guests are treated to a complimentary bottle of wine. There are hiking trails and even a canoe trail on the property. Guests sometimes bring their own canoes. Rachel recommends paddling out Big Creek to the Satilla River, then downstream to Nahunta—a trip of about five hours. Horseback riding is available nearby.

The rustic restaurant is open for dinner Wednesday through Saturday. Beer and wine are available with meals. Reservations are required, especially on weekends.

From US 82 east between Waycross and Brunswick, turn left onto State 121/15. Go one mile and look for an inn sign directing you to turn left. From there the route is clearly marked.

The Helmstead

Jane Helms
One Fargo Road (State 441)
Homerville, GA 31634
912-487-2222

$40–$50 • Open all year • 4 rooms, 1 suite
• Home stay • No kids, no pets, no smoking
• Rating: 3

Cheerful Jane Helms will welcome you with open arms. The Helmstead is her lovely two-story traditional-style home—not old but built with antique bricks. It sits at the edge of town on sweeping, well-manicured lawns at the head of a circular driveway. Flowers spill out of baskets by the front door.

The interior is spotlessly clean and flawlessly decorated. Guests are welcome to use the library, living room, and dining room.

Guest rooms are individually decorated. Two share a bath; the rest have private baths. Bedding sizes vary from twins to doubles. The suite features a sitting room with a TV and phone.

As the classiest accommodation for miles around, The Helmstead is popular with business travelers.

Jane provides a Continental breakfast in her sunny dining room. High tea is served in the afternoon. Jane turns down your bed at night and leaves a chocolate on your pillow. This lovely property boasts a swimming pool and a tennis court, and Jane can recommend the best bass fishing spots. For an extra fee, she will provide transportation to and from the airport.

The Helmstead is located on the left side of US 441/State 89, just south of Homerville.

Goodbread House

Betty and Georga Krauss
209 Osborne Street
Saint Marys, GA 31558
912-882-7490

$60 • Open all year • 4 rooms • Home stay •
No kids, no pets, restricted smoking, no credit
cards • Rating: 3½

The Goodbread House is a 1870 Victorian on the main street of Saint Marys'
historic district. The small landscaped yard sits behind a neat picket fence. During
the inn's long life, it has served as a boardinghouse and restaurant popular with
locals, and as an apartment house. When the previous owners moved into the
house in 1988, they hadn't even thought of opening a B&B. One night a perfect
stranger knocked on the door and asked if the house was a B&B (it looks just like
one). The idea took root and it has been one ever since.

The exterior of the house is enhanced by full-length porches both upstairs
and down. From these porches you can see the town pier and the Cumberland
Island ferry.

The interior is embellished with high ceilings, wide pine floors, seven fireplaces, and intricate moldings, and is furnished with antiques. Each guest room
has a private bath, decorative fireplace, and ceiling fan. All guest rooms are non-
smoking. Smoking is permitted only in the guest lounge.

Betty serves an elegant full breakfast in the formal dining room using her
china and silver. Wine is served to guests at the cocktail hour, and newspapers are
provided.

From I-95 or US 17, take State 40 east. As you enter town, State 40 becomes
Osborne Street. The inn is past Orange Hall on the right.

The Historic Spencer House Inn

Donna and Dale Potruski
101 East Bryant Street
Saint Marys, GA 31558
912-882-1872

$55–$120 • Open all year • 14 rooms • B&B
inn • Kids, no pets, restricted smoking,
provision for disabled • Rating: 4

Built as a hotel in 1872, this lovely pink Victorian has been restored and returned
to its original use. The three-story structure is located in the historic district on the
main street of Saint Marys. Large verandas with ample rockers enhance the front
on both the first and second floors.

Step into the tiny lobby for registration. Selected fabrics and furnishings
breathe new life into the sunny, many-windowed inn. Original moldings and
wide-planked wood floors add warmth and beauty.

Guest rooms are decorated with antiques and period reproductions. Bedding
varies, including twins, doubles, queens, and kings. Each room has a private bath,
with a claw-foot tub or a shower, and each room features a TV, phone, and ceiling
fan. An elevator permits easy access to all three floors.

Conversation areas in the upstairs halls encourage guests to get to know one
another. Business travelers favor the inn, which is suitable for small corporate
meetings.

A Continental breakfast is served buffet style in the upstairs hall. Weather
permitting, the best place to enjoy your breakfast is on one of the verandas. Wine
and cheese are served at cocktail time. For an additional fee, you can request a
picnic lunch; complimentary bicycles are available. Spencer House Inn offers
special golf and Cumberland Island packages and sponsors occasional murder mystery weekends.

From I-95, exit onto State 40. As you enter Saint Marys, State 40 becomes
Osborne Street. The inn is on the left at the corner of Bryant and Osborne.

Little St. Simons Island
Deborah McIntyre
P.O. Box 1078
Saint Simons, GA 31522
912-638-7472

$200-$400 • February 1-November 15 • 12
rooms, 4 cottages • Country inn/resort • Kids
over 6, no pets, restricted smoking, honor bar
• Rating: 5

LITTLE
ST. SIMONS
ISLAND

The private barrier island of Little Saint Simons is accessible only by a twice-daily private ferry. The 10,000-acre island caters to a maximum of only twenty-four guests at a time.

You'll find seven miles of unspoiled beaches that yield fistfuls of sand dollars and other shells. Freely roaming deer, soaring eagles, alligators, armadillos, pristine forests, freshwater ponds, isolated beaches, marshlands, and more than 200 species of birds are the major attractions.

Each paneled lodge includes two or four bedrooms with private bath. Ceiling fans and frequent breezes substitute for air-conditioning. Each common room features a fireplace, games, books, and magazines. There is no radio, TV, or newspapers. One phone in the office permits access to the outside world in emergencies. The newer lodges offer laundry facilities.

This informal island hideaway is ideal for family reunions, small groups, or business conferences. June through September, the island is available only to groups who take the entire complex. In spring and fall—March to May and October to November—the facility is open to individuals, couples, families, and very small groups.

Almost everything—including wine with dinner—is included in the daily rate: $300-$400 per couple, $200-$300 single. A two-night minimum is required. Meals are served family style in the main lodge. Expect afternoon hors d'oeuvres, a cookout, and a beach picnic. The large swimming pool may be the site of snorkeling, canoe, or kayak lessons. Horseback riding is available, as are canoes, kayaks, small motorboats, and fishing gear. Naturalists will take you around the island to identify flora and fauna.

From I-95, take Spur 25 to US 17. Take the F. J. Torras Causeway across to Saint Simons Island. Follow Demere Road and turn left onto Frederica Road. Follow it all the way to the end to remote Hampton Point Marina. Park your car and board a small ferry for the short ride.

118 West
Andrea Walker
118 West Gaston Street
Savannah, GA 31401
912-234-8557

$75-$125 • Open all year • 1 suite/apartment
• Home stay • Kids over 12, no pets, no
smoking • Rating: 4

This beautiful B&B occupies the lower floor of an elegantly restored 1850 town house in Savannah's historic district. Brick walls, exposed beams, and wide-board pine floors enhance the apartment, consisting of a bedroom, living room, dining area, and full kitchen, with phone, cable TV, and fireplaces in both the living room and bedroom. The furnishings, which include a sofa bed and a wicker-canopied sofa, are eclectic, helping guests feel at ease. Guests have access to a charming enclosed courtyard. Parking is on the street—a characteristic problem in the historic district.

As is typical in Savannah B&Bs that are actually apartments, a Continental-plus breakfast of fruit, English muffins, cereal, and juice is left the night before. A coffeemaker and toaster are provided.

I-16 ends and merges into Montgomery Street. Turn right immediately onto Liberty. Go four blocks and turn right onto Whitaker. Go eleven blocks to West Gaston and turn left. The inn is on the right.

17 Hundred 90 Inn
Dick and Darlene Lehmkuhl
307 East President Street
Savannah, GA 31401
912-236-7122 or 800-487-1790

$79–$129 • Open all year • 14 rooms • Country
inn • Kids, no pets, smoking • Rating: 4½

Named for the year in which the foundation was laid, the inn and restaurant recently celebrated its 204th birthday.

You'll be assured luxury, Old South charm, and gracious pampering in the luxuriously appointed guest rooms. High ceilings, antiques, and appropriate fabrics authenticate the flavor of early America. Gas fireplaces add romance to twelve of the rooms.

Eight rooms offer a single bed in addition to the double bed. The extralarge room contains a king-size bed on a step-up platform, a large sitting area, a table and chairs, and a desk. Two special rooms, popular with honeymooners and other romantics, feature mirrors on the ceilings. Business travelers endorse this inn, which is suitable for small corporate meetings.

A Continental-plus breakfast is served in the dining room. Each room has a small refrigerator in which you'll find a welcome bottle of wine.

The entire downstairs is devoted to gastronomic delights, focusing on Continental cuisine and fine wines in the restaurant, which has been in continuous service for thirty-seven years. Low ceilings, brick walls and floors, dim flickering lights, and the glow from the huge twin fireplaces enhance the intimate colonial atmosphere. Accolades include six years of "Silver Spoon" awards from the Gourmet Diners Club.

Try the 17 Hundred 90's Lounge for afternoon and evening cocktails and complimentary hors d'oeuvres (a meal in themselves).

I-16 ends as it merges onto Montgomery Street. Pass the Civic Center on the right and go two more blocks. Turn right onto York. Go seven blocks and turn left onto Lincoln. The inn is at the corner of Lincoln and President.

A Bed & Breakfast

George and Margaret McClellan
221 East Gordon Street
Savannah, GA 31401
912-236-1863

$95 • Open all year • 1 suite • Home stay
• Kids, no pets, no smoking, no credit cards
• Rating: 4

Just as Margaret and George have merged two cultures in their marriage, they have combined the best of British and American hospitality in their bed and breakfast.

The McClellans have developed contemporary living in a historical setting by tasteful renovation of their 1872 town house. Both in their private quarters and in the B&B suite, they've created a spare, modern look by the elimination of architectural details and by the generous use of white. Sleek furnishings and artwork in muted colors enhance the light, airy look.

The suite offers an elegant sitting room looking out onto Calhoun Square as well as a dining nook, fully equipped kitchen, bedroom, and bath. A well-lighted corner is a quiet study area ideal for a business traveler or traveling writer. Extra guests can be accommodated on the queen-size sofa bed.

Breakfast fixings are left in the suite for guests to enjoy at their leisure. You'll find just about anything you could want: cereals, English muffins, croissants, bagels, frozen waffles, home-baked breads, egg substitute, and much more.

The suite features cable TV, a clock radio, and a telephone as well as access to laundry facilities. Guests are encouraged to use the gas grill in the intimate courtyard. Afternoon cocktails are offered. A daily complimentary newspaper is provided.

I-16 ends and merges into Montgomery Street. Turn right almost immediately onto Liberty Street. Go four blocks and turn right onto Whitaker. Go nine blocks and turn left onto Gordon. Just past the Massie Heritage Interpretive Center on the right, you'll see the American and British flags flying at a sign for the inn.

Ballastone Inn & Townhouse

Richard F. Carlson and Timothy C. Hargus
14 East Oglethorpe Avenue
Savannah, GA 31401
912-236-1484 or 800-822-4553 in state

$95–$200 • Open all year • 24 rooms • B&B
inn • Kids over 12, no pets, smoking • Rating: 5

The Tiffany's of Savannah's small hostelries is the luxurious Ballastone Inn, housed in an exquisitely restored 1853 Victorian mansion. It was originally a wealthy shipper's home but has served as an apartment house and even a bordello. The inn has been selected as one of the most romantic inns in the nation by both *Bride's Magazine* and *Glamour*. Additional accommodations are available in an elegant 1830s town house on Liberty Street.

Each of the guest rooms in the main inn reflects a distinct Victorian flavor. The town house offers suites with a kitchen, bedroom with private bath, and sitting room.

The formal atmosphere of the high-ceilinged rooms is enhanced with antiques and period reproductions. Guest rooms are appointed with rice poster and canopy beds, marble-topped tables and dressers, cheval mirrors, comfortable love seats, and wing chairs. The guest rooms on the garden level of the main inn sport country and primitive decor and furnishings.

Every guest room and suite features a private bath, ceiling fan, TV, and VCR. Most rooms have king- or queen-size beds and a working or decorative fireplace. Some rooms are appointed with whirlpool baths and wet bars. The inn has a small charming courtyard and offers an elevator.

Off-street parking is available. Ballastone Inn is favored by business travelers and is suitable for small business conferences. Corporate rates are available.

A Continental breakfast is brought to your room, or you may eat in the parlor or courtyard. Complimentary sherry is always on hand; other cocktails are available on the honor system. Fresh flowers and fruit are placed in the guest rooms. Nightly turn-down service includes a chocolate on your pillow and a liquer beside the bed. Fluffy robes are provided. A library of 150 videos is available.

I-16 ends where it merges into Montgomery Street. Turn right at the second traffic light onto Oglethorpe Avenue. Go four blocks until you pass Bull Street. The inn is on the left in the next block adjacent to the Juliette Gordon Lowe House.

Bed & Bagel

Hanz and Paula Robin
505 East President Street
Savannah, GA 31401
912-236-1122

$80–$125 • Open all year • 1 suite • Kids, no
pets, no smoking • Rating: 3

A whimsical name sets this B&B apart from the more staid and proper Savannah inns. The suite occupies the garden level of an 1854 single house located between Columbia and Greene Squares. Appropriately enough, the original owner was a baker, and several underground ovens remain. Today Paula carries on the baking tradition.

Interior walls are exposed tabby—a building material of limestone, sand, and oyster shells unique to the Georgia coast. The suite consists of a sitting room, bedroom, fully equipped kitchen, breakfast room, and one and a half baths, with decorative fireplaces, ceiling fans, color TV, phone, clock radio, king-size bed, and two daybeds. Furnishings and decor are sparse and contemporary. Weekends have a two-night minimum stay.

As you'd expect from the name, breakfast includes bagels and cream cheese. However, the meal—which can be delivered in the morning or left in the suite for guests to enjoy at their leisure—also consists of cranberry nut bread, pastries, fresh fruit, juice, jellies, and jams.

Bed & Bagel is located at the far eastern extreme of the historic district. Most attractions are within walking distance.

I-16 ends and merges into Montgomery Street. Almost immediately, turn right onto Liberty. Follow it nine blocks to Habersham. Turn left and go nine blocks to President and turn right. The inn is in the middle of the block on the right.

Bed and Breakfast Inn

Robert McCallister
117 and 119 West Gordon Street
Savannah, GA 31401
912-238-0518

$33–$79 • Open all year • 14 rooms • B&B inn
• Kids, pets restricted, restricted smoking
• Rating: 3½

Two 1853 Federal town houses, centrally located overlooking Chatham Square in Savannah's historic district, compose the Bed and Breakfast Inn. A formal atmosphere is created by an eclectic mixture of antiques and artwork. A lovely landscaped courtyard is tucked behind the houses.

Guest accommodations are rooms in the upper stories of the town houses and a garden apartment on the lower level. In addition there are two carriage house apartments. The apartments feature a private entrance, kitchen, living room with queen-size sofa bed, and bedroom with twin or queen-size beds. Decorative fireplaces grace many of the guest rooms—most of which feature queen-size beds, although a few have twins. All have private baths. Both on- and off-street parking is available.

A hearty home-style breakfast is served in the sunny dining room. The lush courtyard is a delightful place to enjoy morning coffee or an evening cocktail. Sherry and mints are provided in the garden apartment.

I-16 ends and merges into Montgomery Street. Turn right almost immediately onto Liberty. Go three blocks and turn right at Barnard. Go seven blocks, passing Pulaski Square. When you get to Chatham Square, turn left onto West Gordon. The inn is on the right in the middle of the block—identified by a tiny sign on the second level.

Comer House

Caroline Hill
2 East Taylor Street
Savannah, GA 31401
912-234-2923 or 800-262-4667

$75-$135 • Open all year • 2 suites • Home stay
• Kids over 12, no pets, no smoking, no credit
cards • Rating: 4

Comer House is a historic 1880 Victorian town house in Savannah's historic district. Jefferson Davis, former president of the Confederacy, stayed here for a week during a tour of the South in 1886.

Accommodations consist of a one-bedroom suite and a two-bedroom suite located on the garden level. Both have a private bath, antiques, polished pine floors, queen-size bed, decorative fireplace, cable TV, and phone. Guests in both suites are encouraged to enjoy the picturesque courtyard.

The one-bedroom suite has an eating area with table and chairs, refrigerator, sink, and coffeemaker. In addition to the two bedrooms, the larger suite has a sitting room, dining room, kitchen, and a large porch. Off-street parking is provided.

A Continental breakfast is left in each suite so guests can eat at their leisure.

I-16 ends and merges into Montgomery Street. Turn right almost immediately onto Liberty Street. Go five blocks and turn right onto Bull. The inn faces Monterey Square.

East Bay Inn

Jean Ryerson
225 East Bay Street
Savannah, GA 31401
912-238-1225 or 800-500-1225

$79–$99 • Open all year • 28 rooms • B&B inn
• Kids, ask about pets, restricted smoking
• Rating: 4

During the 1880s, the building in which the East Bay Inn now resides was a cotton warehouse with offices on the third floor. It was later occupied by a drugstore, then stood empty for many years. In 1984, the building began a new life as a bed and breakfast. Its location just across the street from Emmet Park, Factors Walk, and the attractions of River Street makes it ideal for tourists.

Despite its checkered past, the building retains its original crown molding, hardwood floors, and Savannah bricks. Public areas and guest rooms are furnished with period reproductions, porcelains, antique maps, and artwork by Audubon and Catsby. All guest rooms have private baths, queen-size four-poster beds, armoires, and Oriental rugs. Some rooms are connecting, and some have sofa beds. There is an elevator and off-street parking. East Bay Inn is particularly well suited to business travelers and corporate meetings of up to 100. Corporate rates are available.

A Continental-plus breakfast is included. Limited cocktails, including wine and liqueurs, are offered in the evening, as is a complimentary newspaper. Skler's Restaurant serves Asian/gourmet cuisine. A huge room with brick walls and floor as well as gigantic fireplaces, it can serve meetings and banquets of up to 100.

I-16 ends and merges into Montgomery Street. Pass the Civic Center on the right as well as Elbert, Liberty, and Franklin Squares. Turn right onto West Bay Street. Go seven blocks. The inn is on the right, opposite Emmet Park on the left.

Eliza Thompson Inn

Arthur Smith
5 West Jones Street
Savannah, GA 31401
912-236-3620 or 800-348-9378

$68–$108 • Open all year • 25 rooms, 1 suite
• B&B inn • Kids, no pets, no smoking
• Rating: 4

This elegant 1847 Federal-style town house was built for a red-haired widow named Eliza Thompson. During the Civil War, she lived in fear that Sherman's troops would burn the house. However, when Union soldiers camped in Madison Square, Miss Eliza and other ladies made corn cakes in her kitchen and sold them to the soldiers, enabling her to stay in their good graces and protect her house.

Twelve of the guest rooms are located in the historic town house; thirteen rooms are in a modern addition that blends well with the original. The house and addition are furnished with period reproductions. Heart-pine floors gleam in the original house; floors in the addition are carpeted. Many rooms feature decorative moldings, fireplaces, and Old Savannah colors and patterns. Rooms may feature Charleston rice beds or Federal pencil-post beds. The three garden-level rooms have small refrigerators. Tucked behind the house is a large, beautifully landscaped courtyard with an iron fountain.

Business travelers enjoy staying at the Eliza Thompson House. Corporate rates are available.

A Continental-plus breakfast is served. In good weather, you'll want to take it out to the charming courtyard. Every evening guests gather in the formal parlor for a wine and cheese reception. Complimentary newspapers are provided.

I-16 ends and merges into Montgomery Street. Turn right at the first traffic light onto Liberty Street, then right at the next light onto Whitaker. Go three blocks and turn left onto Jones. The inn is on the right.

Foley House Inn

Susan M. Steinhauser, Innkeeper
Richard Botnick, Owner
14 West Hull Street
Savannah, GA 31401
912-232-6622 or 800-647-3708 out of state

$100–$200 • Open all year • 20 rooms, 1 suite
• B&B inn • Kids, ask about pets, restricted
smoking • Rating: 4

The Foley House Inn occupies an elegant 1896 Victorian town house on Chippewa Square. Restored to the most minute detail, it is furnished with period antiques, hand-colored engravings, and Oriental rugs. The exquisite parlor chandelier is from the set of *Gone With the Wind*, as is a candelabra at the foot of the stairway.

During the 1800s it was believed that gargoyles could ward off evil spirits, so many houses displayed them. At the Foley House, gargoyles adorn several fireplaces.

The house is named for its first owner, Honoria Foley. Some believe that her spirit still dwells in the house. During the restoration of the two houses that make up the inn, a human skeleton was found in the wall between the two. No one has been able to solve the mystery of who it was and how it got there.

The guest rooms in the main house are decorated in Victorian style with four-poster beds, gas fireplaces, and period antiques; many rooms have antique armoires. The rooms in the carriage house are decorated in the country classic look and have small balconies. Beds are either kings or doubles. All rooms have private baths; four offer oversized hot tubs. The Essex Suite takes up almost an entire floor. In addition to the king-size, four-poster canopy bed, the suite contains a daybed, wet bar, wide-screen TV, VCR, Jacuzzi, and a large bay window overlooking the square.

This B&B is suitable for business travelers and small corporate meetings. Corporate rates (and family rates) are available. Ask about parking, which is limited.

A Continental-plus breakfast is served in your room, in the parlor, or on the patio. Complimentary afternoon tea and cocktails with wine and cheese are served in the parlor or in your room.

I-16 ends and merges into Montgomery Street. Immediately after you pass the Civic Center, turn right onto West Oglethorpe. Go three blocks and turn right onto Whitaker. Go two blocks and turn left at West Hull. Foley House is on the northwest corner of Chippewa Square.

Forsyth Park Inn

Virginia and Hal Sullivan
102 West Hall Street
Savannah, GA 31401
912-233-6800

$85–$145 • Open all year • 9 rooms, 1 cottage
• B&B inn • Kids, no pets, smoking • Rating: 4

The inn occupies a restored Queen Anne mansion overlooking Forsyth Park—Savannah's largest and most opulent square. The house has sixteen-foot ceilings and ornate wood details and is elegantly decorated with antiques, including a grand piano in the parlor.

Guest rooms feature period furnishings, four-poster king- and queen-size beds, fireplaces, antique marble baths, and carefully preserved architectural details. Four guest rooms offer Jacuzzis. The cottage has a kitchen. There are no phones.

A Continental-plus breakfast buffet is laid out in the parlor, or you may want to eat in the courtyard. Port and sherry are always available in the parlor.

Forsyth Park has jogging paths, tennis courts, and playgrounds.

I-16 ends and merges with Montgomery Street. Turn right almost immediately onto Liberty Street, then right again onto Whitaker. The inn is in the second block after you see Forsyth Park on the left.

The Gastonian

Roberta and Hugh Lineberger
220 East Gaston Street
Savannah, GA 31401
912-232-2869 or 800-322-6603 or
FAX 912-232-0710

$115–$275 • Open all year • 10 rooms, 3 suites
• B&B inn • Kids over 12, no pets, no
smoking, provision for disabled • Rating: 5

The Gastonian is one of the most outstanding and glamorous B&Bs we've seen anywhere. *Hideaway Report* has named it one of the top ten B&Bs in the country. Mobil has awarded the inn four stars, and AAA has honored it with five diamonds.

Two sumptuous, exquisitely revitalized 1868 town houses are connected by a graceful garden courtyard. The owners live on the property—unusual for a Savannah B&B—and the difference shows. Guest accommodations have high ceilings, heart-pine floors, Oriental carpets, decorative moldings, brass, traditional Old Savannah Scalamandre wallpaper, and antiques of the Georgian and Regency periods. All rooms have private baths (nine have either soak tubs or whirlpools), gas fireplaces, air-conditioning, king- or queen-size beds, color TVs, and telephones. The penthouse can also be used as a hospitality suite, and the Caracalla Suite makes an idyllic honeymoon or anniversary getaway. There is a large Jacuzzi on a deck in the garden area.

In a quiet residential area of the historic district, the inn has plenty of off-street parking. It is popular with business travelers and particularly well suited for small corporate meetings. Corporate rates are available.

A generous full southern breakfast is served in the ornate dining room, or a silver-service Continental breakfast can be served in your room. Formal afternoon tea is served in the parlor, and complimentary wine, flowers, and fruit await you in your room.

I-16 ends and merges onto Montgomery Street. Turn right almost immediately onto Liberty Street. Go five blocks and turn right at Bull Street. Pass both Madison and Monterey Squares, then turn left onto East Gaston. The inn is on the left at the corner of East Gaston and Lincoln.

Joan's on Jones

Joan Levy
17 West Jones Street
Savannah, GA 31401
912-234-3863

$85–$95 • Open all year • 2 suites • Home stay
• Kids, ask about pets, no smoking, no credit
cards • Rating: 4

Many of Savannah's B&Bs are suites located on the lower level of gracious town houses. Joan has improved on the concept by making the garden level of her 1883 Victorian into two different-sized connecting accommodations. Together or separately, they are ideal for families, couples, or groups traveling together.

The sitting area of the smaller suite, off the walled garden, is furnished in white wicker with gaily colored floral prints. The bedroom features a queen-size white iron bed and a decorative fireplace. The kitchen is fully equipped.

The larger, more formal suite has a sitting room with decorative fireplace and a queen-size sofa bed, a bedroom with an opulent four-poster rice bed, and a minikitchen. Both suites have a private bath, private entry, off-street parking, period antiques, TV, and access to the courtyard. Rollaway beds can be provided. Business travelers or those making a long-term stay are welcome.

A Continental breakfast basket is left in your suite. Wine and fruit are served at cocktail time.

When I-16 ends, it merges into Montgomery Street. Turn right almost immediately onto Liberty, then right again at Barnard. Turn left onto Jones. The house, on the right, is identified by a discreet sign near the curb.

The Kehoe House
Peggy Holmes
123 Habersham Street
Savannah, GA 31401
912-232-1020 or 800-820-1020 or
FAX 912-231-0208

$150–$225 • Open all year • 13 rooms, 2 suites
• B&B hotel • No kids, no pets, no smoking
• Rating: 5

Recently restored, this magnificent Victorian mansion on Columbia Square was unusual as a single house in turn-of-the-century Savannah when town houses were the norm. Listed on the National Register of Historic Places, Kehoe House now operates as a luxurious European-style inn with sumptuous guest rooms, elegant public spaces, a huge private boardroom, and an executive fitness area. Although open only since January 1993, the inn has been awarded four diamonds by AAA. Next door is a small restored town house with two sumptuous suites.

Guest rooms in the main inn are furnished with antiques and reproductions. All feature private baths and some have private entrances onto the upstairs porches. An elevator provides access to the upper floors. The entire fourth floor is utilized as a conference room. Tucked into a cranny is a small boardroom. Kehoe House offers full secretarial services, making the property ideal for business travelers and small corporate meetings.

A full gourmet breakfast is served in the dining room. Rates include an English afternoon tea and hors d'oeuvres. A well-stocked bar is operated on the honor system.

When I-16 ends, it merges onto Montgomery Street. Pass the Civic Center on the right and go two more blocks. Turn right onto York. Go seven blocks and turn left onto Lincoln. The inn is at the corner of Habersham and President.

Lion's Head Inn

Christy Dell'Orco
120 East Gaston Street
Savannah, GA 31401
912-232-4580 or 800-355-LION or
FAX 912-232-7422

$85–$135 • Open all year • 4 rooms, 2 suites
• B&B inn • Kids, no pets, restricted smoking
• Rating: 4

A gleaming brass lion's head greets you. Situated in a large 1883 Federal-style house, the inn features hand-carved marble mantels, detailed wood and plaster moldings, Savannah gray bricks, and hardwood floors. As a result of the Dell'Orcos' fifteen years of accumulating art and antiques, the inn is decorated with nineteenth-century Empire furnishings and an admirable collection of F. Romanelli marble sculpture.

Guest rooms have private baths and are furnished with American Federal antiques. All but one room offers a king- or queen-size four-poster bed, gas fireplace, phone, and cable TV with HBO.

Two cozy rooms on the garden level feature exposed brick walls and beamed ceilings. The Natchez Suite has a bedroom with a king-size bed and a sitting room with a queen-size sofa bed. The Savannah Suite features two large bedrooms with queen-size beds and an antique bathroom with a claw-foot tub. A spacious walled courtyard, brimming with azaleas, is elegantly furnished with white wicker and wrought iron. The gracious public rooms and courtyard are ideal for weddings, receptions, and luncheons. There is ample off-street parking.

A Continental-plus breakfast is served in the dining room or on the veranda. Rates include afternoon tea and evening Savannah sweets and brandy.

I-16 ends and merges into Montgomery Street. Turn right immediately onto Liberty. Go four blocks and turn right onto Whitaker. Go eleven blocks to West Gaston. Turn left and the inn is on the right.

Magnolia Place Inn

Ronald Strong
503 Whitaker Street
Savannah, GA 31401
912-236-7674 or 800-238-7674 out of state

$89-$195 • Open all year • 13 rooms • B&B
inn • Kids, smoking, reservations required
• Rating: 4

Ideally located in Savannah's historic district and overlooking Forsyth Park, Magnolia Place Inn retains the graceful ambience of the original mansion, built in 1878. The Victorian inn features both a first-floor and second-floor veranda facing the park. Tall windows capture afternoon breezes. The magnificent two-story foyer is set off by parquet floors and inlaid marquetry and is crowned by a stained-glass window thirty feet above. Tiles painted for the house ornament two of the twelve working fireplaces, all with original mantles. A collector's cabinet in the parlor houses a butterfly collection that spans two generations.

Guest rooms are furnished with English antiques, period prints, and porcelains from around the world. The rooms on the lower level are furnished in a more casual style than those upstairs. All rooms have private baths and king- or queen-size beds—many with canopies and side draperies. Each room has a TV and VCR. Six rooms feature Jacuzzis and all but two have gas fireplaces. There is a hot tub in the enclosed courtyard.

A Continental breakfast is brought to your room, or you may eat in the parlor or on the porch or patio. Afternoon tea and cocktails are served. You can borrow from the large library of videotapes. This inn has off-street parking, and there are tennis courts across the street in Forsyth Park. A honeymoon package includes champagne, fresh flowers, and a carriage tour of the city. Corporate and group rates are available.

When I-16 ends, it merges onto Montgomery Street. Turn right almost immediately onto Liberty Street. Go four blocks and turn right at Whitaker. Go eleven blocks. The inn faces the northwest corner of Forsyth Park.

Olde Harbour Inn

Jean Ryerson
508 East Factors Walk
Savannah, GA 31401
912-234-4100 or 800-553-6533

$95–$145 • Open all year • 24 suites • B&B inn
• Kids, ask about pets, smoking • Rating: 4

Built in 1892, the Olde Harbour Inn is rich in River Street history. The three-story building was originally the offices, warehouse, and shipping center of the Tide Water Oil Company. Unusual facets of the construction are beams fashioned from various parts of old sailing vessels and gray bricks that were the first compressed ones used in Savannah.

Every accommodation is really an apartment, with a fully equipped kitchen, living room and dining area furnished in period reproductions, and a bedroom or sleeping loft. All suites overlook the river; a few have a small balcony.

The inn is appealing to business travelers making long-term stays and is suitable for small corporate meetings.

A Continental-plus breakfast buffet is served in the sunny Marine Room. At cocktail hour, guests gather in the Grand Salon for wine, sherry, and hors d'oeuvres accompanied by classical music and candlelight. The comfortably furnished library offers books, magazines, and newspapers. Nightly turn-down service includes ice cream left in the freezer.

I-16 ends and merges into Montgomery Street. Go past the Civic Center on the right, as well as Elbert, Liberty, and Franklin Squares. Turn right onto West Bay Street. Go ten blocks and turn left onto the Lincoln Ramp. Follow the ramp down and turn right onto Factors Walk. The inn's entrance is on the left. Park your car up on East Bay Street.

Planters Inn

Tricia Patterson
29 Abercorn Street
Savannah, GA 31401
912-232-5678 or 800-554-1187

$89–$125 • Open all year • 56 rooms • B&B
hotel/resort • Kids, no pets, smoking restricted,
provision for disabled • Rating: 4

Restored to its 1912 beauty, Planters Inn has returned to its original purpose—to serve as an elegant hotel in the heart of Savannah's historic district.

The hotel's sumptuous pink marble lobby, which serves as a gathering place for breakfast and afternoon tea, has intricate moldings, soaring columns, and immense gilt-framed mirrors; it is elegantly furnished with comfortable sofas and wing chairs. The guest rooms—all with private bath—feature high ceilings, period reproductions, and Old Savannah-style upholstery and draperies.

A Continental breakfast buffet is set out in the lobby each morning, or a more elaborate breakfast is available from room service at an additional cost. Tea served each afternoon in the lobby includes hot beverages and generous helpings of cake or other dessert. Newspapers are delivered to each room in the morning. There is valet parking, bicycle rental, and access to an athletic club. Conference facilities, hospitality suites, and secretarial services are available.

I-16 ends and merges into Montgomery Street. Go past the Civic Center on the right, as well as Elbert, Liberty, and Franklin Squares. Turn right onto West Bay Street. Go six blocks and turn right on Abercorn. The inn faces Reynolds Square.

Presidents' Quarters

Muril L. Broy
225 East President Street
Savannah, GA 31401
912-233-1600 or 800-233-1776

$97–$157 • Open all year • 9 rooms, 7 suites
• B&B inn • Kids, no pets, restricted smoking,
provision for disabled, reservations preferred
• Rating: 4½

On our way to an overnight stay at Presidents' Quarters, we had car trouble and didn't get in until midnight. The night staff lit our fireplace and served us tea, cakes, and a liqueur. That's the kind of pampering you can expect here.

This mirrored pair of Greek Revival brick town houses, built in 1855 in Savannah's historic district, was the backdrop for the slave sale scene in *Roots*.

First-floor rooms are outfitted for the disabled. The fourth floor offers loft suites. Each room is dedicated to a president, with portraits, photos, newspaper clippings, handwritten notes, or other memorabilia. Rooms feature reproduction furniture, gas fireplaces, ceiling fans, Jacuzzi tubs, terry-cloth robes, cable TV, VCR, and queen-size sofa beds. Some rooms have a balcony or a courtyard. There is a splash pool and an outdoor heated hot tub. Ask about the deluxe Honeymoon Package.

Presidents' Quarters is popular with business travelers and offers corporate rates and hospitality suites; it can handle small meetings and conferences.

A Continental-plus breakfast is served in your room or the formal parlor, or on the enclosed patio. A full afternoon tea as well as cocktails and hors d'oeuvres are served daily in the lobby. There are complimentary newspapers, valet service, and off-street parking.

I-16 ends and merges into Montgomery Street. Go two blocks past the Civic Center and turn right onto York. Go six blocks to Oglethorpe Square. Just past the square, turn left. The inn is on the east side of the square at President Street.

Pulaski Square Inn
J. B. Smith
203 West Charlton Street
Savannah, GA 31401
912-232-8055 or 800-227-0650

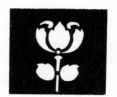

$48-$198 • Open all year • 5 rooms, 3 suites
• B&B inn • Kids, no pets, smoking, provision
for disabled • Rating: 4

Built in 1853, this restored town house and accompanying carriage house overlook Pulaski Square in Savannah's historic district. Interior embellishments include marble mantles, heart-pine floors, Oriental carpets, and antique furniture.

Guest rooms are appointed with decorative fireplaces, and most feature king- or queen-size beds. The elegant Honeymoon Suite features twelve-foot ceilings, a sitting room, a fully equipped kitchen, a queen-size four-poster bed, antiques, Oriental rugs, a working fireplace, Scalamandre draperies, old English brass, marble mantles, and gold-leaf mirrors. The unusual bathroom fixtures include ornate gold-plated swans. In addition to the guest rooms in the main house, the carriage house sleeps six.

Guests can enjoy the courtyard and garden. Off-street parking, an elevator, and corporate rates are available.

You may choose to have your Continental-plus breakfast in your room, the kitchen, or the third-floor butler's pantry.

I-16 ends and merges into Montgomery Street. Turn right almost immediately onto Liberty Street. Go two blocks and turn right at Tattnall. Go three blocks and turn left at West Charlton. The inn is on the right in the first block.

Remshart-Brooks House

Anne Barnett
106 West Jones Street
Savannah, GA 31401
912-234-6928

$75–$115 • Open all year • 1 suite • Home stay
• Kids over 12, no pets, smoking, no credit
cards • Rating: 4

You could consider this terrace garden suite a home away from home. Located in an 1853 town house in the heart of the historic district, the suite is actually a fully equipped three-room apartment furnished in Virginia and Georgia country antiques.

The suite—which has a private entrance—offers a sitting room with exposed beams and brick walls, a fireplace, comfortable seating, a sofa bed, an antique game table, a TV, and a dining area. Brass and wicker as well as another fireplace embellish the romantic bedroom. The kitchen is fully equipped. The suite opens onto a gorgeous courtyard, and there is covered off-street parking—a rarity in the historic district.

A Continental-plus breakfast is left in the refrigerator. Two bicycles are available for guests' use, as are an iron and ironing board.

I-16 ends and merges onto Montgomery Street. At the first traffic light, turn right onto Liberty Street. Go three blocks to the next traffic light and turn right onto Whitaker Street. Go five blocks to Jones Street and turn right. The house is the second on the right and is identified by a discreet sign.

River Street Inn

Michael Brandon
115 East River Street
Savannah, GA 31401
912-234-6400 or 800-253-4229

$79-$250 • Open all year • 44 rooms • B&B
hotel/resort • Kids, small pets, smoking,
provision for disabled • Rating: 4

An eighteenth-century cotton warehouse overlooking the Savannah River has been beautifully restored and converted to this gracious hotel. Many rooms have windows or balconies overlooking the river and River Street. Others survey Factors Walk, Emmet Park, and Savannah's historic district.

Inside you'll find gleaming pine floors, intricate moldings, and exposed brick. Furnishings are period reproductions and antiques. Guest room decor ranges from sea captain to English chintz. All rooms have a private bath, color TV, and phone. Many have queen-size beds and decorative fireplaces. The hotel even features a billiard room. Ask about parking. The five-story structure has an elevator. Room rates are for single occupancy. Each additional guest in the same room is $10 extra. The hotel is ideal for business travelers and small- to mid-sized corporate meetings. There are conference facilities for groups up to 150. Secretarial assistance is available. Corporate, group, and weekly rates are offered.

A New Orleans-style Continental breakfast featuring beignets is served at Huey's, located on the lower level. Guests show their room key to be served. At cocktail time wine is served along with fruit and cheese.

The inn is easily accessible from I-16 and I-95 as well as US 17 and US 17A via Montgomery Street. Turn right at West Bay Street and go one-half mile to the gazebo in Emmet Park. The inn is on the left, with its entrance and parking on the Bay Street level.

St. Julian Street Bed & Breakfast

Bill, Judy, and Eric Strong
501 East St. Julian Street
Savannah, GA 31401
912-236-9939

$55–$65 • Open all year • 2 rooms • Home stay
• Kids, ask about pets, restricted smoking, no
credit cards • Rating: 3

Located between Warren and Washington Squares, this B&B is one of the closest to the attractions on River Street. Housed in a Victorian single house, the inn is furnished with antiques. High ceilings and tall windows create a cheerful, airy atmosphere.

The Strongs offer two guest rooms with a shared bath. The quaint bathroom has an old-fashioned water closet and a claw-foot tub with a shower.

A Continental breakfast is served, which you may eat in bed or the formal dining room. Beer and wine are available in the refrigerator. Guests are free to put their items in the refrigerator as well.

The Strongs invite you to relax in their parlor and enjoy the TV and VCR. A balcony and two small courtyards invite guests outdoors.

When I-16 ends, it merges into Montgomery Street. Follow it past the Civic Center on the right as well as Elbert, Liberty, and Franklin Squares. Turn right onto West Bay Street. Go nine long blocks and turn right onto Price Street. Go three blocks. The B&B is on the southwest corner of Price and St. Julian.

Timmons House

Gloria Timmons Stover
407 East Charlton Street
Savannah, GA 31401
912-233-4456

$65 • Open all year • 1 suite • Home stay
• Kids, no pets, no smoking, no credit cards
• Rating: 3½

Timmons House offers a gracious garden-level apartment in a restored 1876 town house facing Troup Square, in Savannah's historic district.

Guests might decide not to leave, because it would be so easy to live in the charming apartment, which features brick walls, a beamed ceiling, a decorative fireplace, hardwood and slate floors, a sofa bed, a TV, and a full kitchen. The rate is $65 for two people. Extra guests in the same room are charged $10.

A Continental breakfast of cereal, muffins, rolls, and croissants is left in the apartment so guests can enjoy it at their leisure. Fixings are available for tea and coffee. Sherry is served on arrival and a fruit basket is left in the apartment.

Guests are invited to relax in the landscaped courtyard. A washer and dryer are available for guests' use.

I-16 ends and merges into Montgomery Street. Turn right almost immediately onto Liberty Street. Go four blocks and turn right onto Whitaker. Go three blocks and turn left onto West Charlton. After you cross Bull, the street becomes East Charlton. The inn is on the right.

Hunter House
John Hunter
1701 Butler Avenue
Tybee Island, GA 31328
912-786-7515

$45-$100 • Open all year • 2 rooms, 2 suites
• Country inn • Kids, no pets, smoking
• Rating: 3

Hunter House is a restored 1910 beach house located one block off the Atlantic Ocean and only twenty minutes from Savannah's historic district. The inn's claim to fame is its second-floor restaurant and lounge, which are open every weeknight and for Sunday brunch.

The guest rooms are very simple. You can tell they were created by a home handyman rather than by a professional. The furnishings are an eclectic mix of many styles. Each room features a private bath, queen-size bed, cable TV, air-conditioning, and an outside entrance. One suite offers a sitting room with a sofa bed. The other suite has a kitchen, working fireplace, microwave, and refrigerator. Utensils are available on request.

John sets out in the kitchen a simple breakfast of juice, hot pastries, toast, and cereal so guests can enjoy it at their leisure. You may decide to eat in the dining room or on one of the porches. You'll enjoy the view and the sea breezes from the second-floor porch as well as having the convenience of a restaurant and lounge on the property. The beach is only a block away for sunbathing, swimming, and fishing. Tennis is available nearby.

Because this is a beach location, there are in-season and off-season rates. The high season runs from Memorial Day through Labor Day and includes St. Patrick's Day weekend. Family rates are available.

From Savannah's historic district, take the President Street extension. It becomes Island Expressway and merges into US 80. Once on Tybee Island it becomes Butler Avenue—the only major street. Continue through the commercial district. When the road forks (at an Arby's), take the left fork. The inn is just ahead on the right.

4

Historic Heartland

The Historic Heartland region is filled with reminders of the Old South. This is *Gone With the Wind* country—many antebellum plantations and town houses survive. We suggest exploring the area by following one of its trails. The ninety-mile **Peach Blossom Trail** follows US 341/41 from its northern end at Jonesboro to Perry in the south. The **Antebellum Trail** is a 117-mile route along State 129/441 from Athens in the north to Macon in the south.

The **Antebellum Trail**—represented by "Auntie Bellum," the silhouette of an 1800s lady—is a treasure trove of southern architecture, museums, and historic sites. Begin at either end, but allow about three days to explore.

Macon—the City of White Columns and Cherry Blossoms—boasts six historic districts. Notable buildings include the **Hay House**, the **Old Cannonball House**, the **Sidney Lanier Cottage**, the **Harriet Tubman Historical and Cultural Museum**, the **Museum of Arts and Sciences**, and the 1884 **Grand Opera House**. Numerous tours, including horse-and-buggy-drawn rides, are available.

Nearby is the **Ocmulgee National Monument Indian Mounds**, which chronicle 12,000 years of history. The site includes a visitors center and museum, ceremonial mounds, and nature trails.

Up State 129 is **Old Clinton** with its early-1800s appearance. Tours with or without guides are available.

In **Milledgeville**, Georgia's capital from 1804 to 1868, you can tour the **Old Governor's Mansion**, the **Museum and Archives of Georgia Education**, the **Old State Capitol Museum**, and several historic homes. The easiest and most entertaining way to inspect the city is by trolley tour. Close by are **Lake Sinclair** and the **Lockerly Arboretum**. In addition to its nature trails, the arboretum features a museum of antique farm implements.

Eatonton was the childhood home of Uncle Remus creator Joel Chandler Harris. Visit the **Brer Rabbit Statue** and the **Uncle Remus Museum and Park**.

Madison, known as "the town Sherman refused to burn," contains a sizable historic district, with **Heritage Hall** and the **Madison-Morgan Cultural Center**. Unfortunately, the historic homes are open to visitors only during the May and December home tours. **Lake Oconee** and **Hard Labor Creek State Park** are close by.

65

Watkinsville was rejected as the site of the University of Georgia because the presence of the **Eagle Tavern** made the town "too frivolous" for young men to study. The restored tavern—a late 1700s stage stop and store—now serves as Watkinsville's Welcome Center and museum. Nearby is **Elder Mill Bridge**, a rare covered bridge still in use on a public road.

Athens claims the first state-chartered university and the first garden club in the nation. Begin with the welcome center, located in 1820 **Church/Waddel/ Brumby House**, the city's oldest surviving structure. Visit historic homes such as the **Taylor-Grady House**, an 1840 Greek Revival mansion. On the grounds of the **University of Georgia** are the **Founders Memorial Garden** and the **State Museum of Art**. While in Athens also visit the **U.S. Navy Supply Corps Museum**, the **State Botanical Garden**, and **Butts-Mehre Heritage Hall**—a sports museum.

If you begin at the northern end of the **Peach Blossom Trail**, you'll be just south of Atlanta Hartsfield International Airport. **Jonesboro** offers two majestic historic homes in the *Gone With the Wind* tradition—**Ashley Oaks** and **Stately Oaks Mansion**. Could Margaret Mitchell have gotten her inspiration here? Actually she did some research at the courthouse.

Hampton is home to the **Atlanta Motor Speedway**. **Barnesville**— known as the buggy capital of the world—features walking tours of the historic district, including **Barnesville Hardware**, former showroom of the Smith Buggy Company. **Forsyth** has a commercial historic district, a **Confederate Cemetery**, and the **Whistle Stop Museum**.

At **Jarrell Plantation** near **Juliette**, you can get insight into farm life between 1840 and 1940 by observing the outbuildings and farm animals. **Fort Valley** is home to the **Massee Lane Gardens**—headquarters of the American Camellia Society. In addition to spring camellias, the garden blooms throughout the year. Here also is the world's largest collection of Edward Marshall Boehm porcelains. The **Museum of Aviation** at Robins Air Force Base in **Warner Robins** exhibits historic aircraft.

Perry, the southern end of the Peach Blossom Trail, is also the northern end of the Andersonville Trail. Taking that route will lead you off on another adventure, but we'll save that for the Presidential Pathways section.

Hardeman-Hutchens House

Paul and Jane Hutchens
5335 Lexington Road
Athens, GA 30605
706-353-1855

$40-$48 • Open all year • 3 rooms • Home stay
• Kids not encouraged, no pets, no smoking,
reservations required, no credit cards
• Rating: 3½

"I want guests to feel as comfortable as if they were Aunt Millie coming to visit," Jane says, and everything about this B&B reflects her philosophy.

The circa 1855 farmhouse is situated on a sixty-acre horse and pony farm just a few minutes from Athens and the University of Georgia. The house, with a formal and an informal parlor downstairs as well as a sitting room in the upstairs hall, is filled with antiques and a profusion of family memorabilia. Guest rooms have a decorative fireplace and a ceiling fan. Bedding varies—twins, a double, and a king. Extra accommodations can be provided on the queen-size sofa bed in the game room. All the guest rooms share one bath. Featured in the upstairs den are a TV and a game table as well as games, books, and magazines. Rooms are $40 single and $48 double. Ask about corporate and family rates.

A full breakfast is served in the dining room.

The property is a bed and breakfast for horses too, and the corner store is now a tack and saddle shop.

Take US 78 east from Athens. The inn is located on the left five miles out of town. Turn left just before the Tack and Saddle Shop and immediately right into the driveway.

Rivendell

Dan and Nancy Connell
3581 South Barnett Shoals Road
Watkinsville, GA 30677
706-769-4522

$50–$65 • Open all year • 4 rooms • Home stay
• Kids over 12, no pets, no smoking • Rating: 3

A newly constructed English-style country house offers its guests architecture of the past and amenities of the present. Eight miles from Athens, the stone house is situated on five heavily wooded acres overlooking the Oconee River.

The interior features a huge living/dining room with a beamed cathedral ceiling and a massive stone fireplace. Enormous windows on the side walls and surrounding the fireplace allow sunlight to pour in. Furnishings include art and antiques from around the world.

A more informal great room downstairs is available to guests. It also has a massive fireplace, TV, and VCR. Compact guest rooms, located on the lower level, are simply furnished in period reproductions. Some guest rooms have a private bath; others share. Family rates are available.

A full breakfast of grits, eggs, biscuits, muffins, bacon, and sausage is served in the great room. The Connells maintain a movie library for the VCR.

Good fishing and golf are available nearby; the Green Hills golf course is less than a mile away.

Take US 441/129 to Watkinsville. Turn east onto Barnett Shoals Road. Go five miles and look for the mailbox on the left. If you get to the Oconee River, you've gone too far.

A Country Place

Barbara and Tommy Jones
Highway 18
Forsyth, GA 30229
912-994-2705

$50 • Open all year • 5 rooms • B&B inn
• Kids over 6, no smoking, provision for
disabled, reservations required, no credit cards
• Rating: 3½

Set amid tranquil pastures, fruit and pecan orchards, and rustic barns, A Country Place is an authentic farmhouse built in 1854. The house is constructed of solid yellow pine held together by pegs and square nails. Hand-hewn marks remain evident on the exposed original walls. The rafters are still numbered with Roman numerals. Nicely restored but retaining its provincial flavor, the B&B has five guest rooms with private baths.

The house has thirteen-foot ceilings, tongue-and-groove walls, pine floors, hand-carved moldings, Shaker rails, a spiral staircase, and gas fireplaces. Each guest room is decorated in antiques and country memorabilia. Brass and iron beds, buttermilk paint-finished tables, ladder-back chairs, and lace curtains enhance the country charm. Four baths feature claw-foot tubs. Two rooms offer a double and a single bed. There is a Jacuzzi on the enclosed back porch. Add $10 to the quoted rate for each extra person.

A Continental breakfast is served. Country dinners can be ordered upon request at an additional fee.

A fascinating feature of the house is a sixty-foot-deep well on the back porch. It was hand-dug by slaves, who laid the solid rock walls and bottom. It is lighted so guests can appreciate the work that went into its construction.

Children and adults will be fascinated by the Jones' ostriches.

From I-75, take exit 60 and turn east on State 18. A Country Place is 2.6 miles on the left.

The Evans-Cantrell House

Cyriline and Norman Cantrell
300 College Street
Fort Valley, GA 31030
912-825-0611

$50–$65 • Open all year • 5 rooms • B&B inn
• Kids over 10, no pets, restricted smoking
• Rating: 3½

A. J. Evans was known as the "Peach King" in both Georgia and South Carolina. The tycoon and philanthropist built his home—an Italian Renaissance Revival mansion—in 1916 in what is now designated as the Everett Square Historic District.

The features that were high tech in 1916 remain today—an electric bell system that could be activated from any room in the house, lighted closets with an automatic switch in the door casing, a central vacuum system, and a shower in the master bedroom that provides water spray both vertically and horizontally or separately.

The Cantrells—second owners of the 6,100-square-foot mansion—have renovated without changing the elegant interior or the honey-colored brick exterior. Plentiful windows and French doors keep the house feeling cheerful and airy. The only room updated to the nineties is the immense kitchen, and two baths have been added. The Evans-Cantrell House has been awarded three diamonds by AAA.

Downstairs the house features a greeting room, parlor, library, formal dining room, and breakfast room, with high ceilings, hardwood floors, mahogany paneling, and original chandeliers and wall sconces. The ornately carved marble fireplace in the parlor is similar to one found in England's Windsor Castle.

Spacious guest rooms have private or shared baths and queen-size beds or doubles. All guest rooms have a desk.

The vast public rooms and 1,000-square-foot porch make the house ideal for small corporate meetings, weddings, and luncheons. Ask about family and corporate rates.

A Continental or full breakfast is served in the sunny informal breakfast room. Guests can use the refrigerator in the butler's pantry for their own items.

From I-75, take the Fort Valley exit (exit 44) west onto State 96. As you enter town, turn left on South Camellia Boulevard, then right onto College Street. The house is at the far-right corner of College and Miller.

1842 Inn

Phillip Jenkins and Richard Meils
353 College Street
Macon, GA 31201
912-741-1842 or 800-336-1842

$79–$109 • Open all year • 21 rooms • B&B
inn • Kids over 10, no pets, restricted smoking,
provision for disabled • Rating: 4½

Considered one of the best-preserved antebellum Greek Revival mansions in the South, the white-columned 1842 inn sits proudly in one of Macon's historic districts. The restored mansion is the recipient of the Georgia Trust for Historic Preservation's Outstanding Restoration Project Award for Adaptive Use Restoration, and has been awarded four diamonds by AAA.

The main house contains formal parlors and a library as well as thirteen guest rooms. In the public rooms, crystal and brass chandeliers sparkle above antique furnishings, elaborate mantels, parquet floors, and Oriental carpets. An additional nine rooms are situated in a two-story Victorian cottage. A pleasant patio fills the area between the two buildings.

Guest rooms are decorated in antiques and period reproductions. Some have Jacuzzis, working fireplaces, and king- or queen-size beds. A few rooms have twin beds. All are air-conditioned and have ceiling fans and TVs.

The inn is ideal for business travelers and small- to mid-sized corporate meetings.

A Continental breakfast is brought on a silver tray in your room along with a bouquet of fresh flowers and the morning newspaper. Wine is sold in the library at cocktail time.

From I-75, take exit 52 onto US Branch 41. Proceed east and turn left onto College Street. The inn is on the left. From I-16, exit onto Spring Street. Proceed south and turn left onto Walnut, then left onto College. The inn is on the right.

The Boat House
Non-Smokers' Bed & Breakfast

Rhonda and Ron Erwin
383 Porter Street Madison, GA 30650
706-342-3061

$75 • Open all year • 4 rooms • Home stay
• No kids, no pets, no smoking, reservations
required, no credit cards • Rating: 4½

Built in 1850 by sea captain Nelson Dexter, this authentically restored house is located on more than an acre of land in Madison's historic district. A bamboo hedge shields the property from the street, and the grounds are abundantly planted with mature trees, ivy, wisteria, and azaleas. A fish pond and a rambling Victorian perennial garden complete the landscape. Both wildlife and guests find a haven here.

The house contains more than 6,000 square feet and boasts gleaming hardwood floors, eleven-foot ceilings, intricate moldings, and ten fireplaces. Guests are invited to use the two first-floor parlors, formal dining room, downstairs and upstairs sunrooms, and upstairs library. The energetic innkeepers own an antique shop, and the house is furnished with a magnificent collection of Victoriana. Many of the items are for sale.

Guest rooms have decorative fireplaces. Two rooms have private baths; two other rooms share a bath. All the baths have claw-foot tubs. An extra bathroom off the library has a shower. Two of the rooms can be combined with small adjoining rooms to create suites. Rates are $75 single and double for a room with private bath. For the suites, each additional guest is $25. Corporate rates are available.

Breakfast is a hearty meal served in the dining room. A less formal meal is served in one of the bright sunrooms or on the wicker-filled porch. Desserts are offered in the evening.

The library contains a large selection of books as well as a TV, VCR, selection of movies, and small refrigerator stocked with soft drinks.

US 441/129 is also Main Street within the city limits. When Main Street crosses Central Avenue, turn west on Central. Go one block to Abernathy Street and turn left. Go two blocks and turn right onto Porter Street. The Boat House is the second house on the right.

Brady Inn

Chris and Lynn Rasch
250 North Second Street
Madison, GA 30650
706-342-4400

$55-$150 • Open all year • 6 rooms, 1 suite
• Country inn • Kids, pets, smoking, provision
for disabled • Rating: 4

The Brady Inn occupies two connected Victorian cottages. One was built in 1895, the other in 1910. Encircled by porches with numerous comfortable rockers, the inn encourages visitors to enjoy the out-of-doors.

Inside are high-ceilinged rooms and suites, stained glass, intricate moldings, pine floors, antiques, and working fireplaces. The large central hall—well stocked with books and magazines—provides an excellent gathering place for guests. Each guest room is decorated in antiques and has double or queen-size beds. All rooms have private baths. The suite offers a sitting room. Family rates are available. The B&B is suitable for business travelers and small corporate meetings.

A full breakfast is served in the dining room. Beer and wine can be purchased. The inn operates a restaurant open for lunch. Dinner groups are served by advance reservation only.

Within the city limits, US 441/129 is Main Street. From Main Street, turn west on either Thomason or Burney and go one block. The inn is on Second Avenue between the two streets.

Burnett Place

Ruth and Leonard Wallace
317 Old Post Road
Madison, GA 30650
706-342-4034

$60–$75 • Open all year • 3 rooms • Home stay
• Kids, no pets, smoking • Rating: 4

Slave built, this circa 1830 house is a two-story Federal-style dwelling typical of the Piedmont region. Before restoring the house, the Wallaces did extensive research. Leonard, an interior designer, worked closely with the Madison Historic Preservation Commission to match the original colors and/or finishes. A glass panel in a wall allows guests to examine the original methods used in the construction of the house.

The decor is a stunning mix of traditional accented with contemporary artwork. Guest rooms have a double bed, private bath, and TV. Two have working fireplaces. Rooms are provided with fluffy bathrobes, a coffeemaker, and fixings for hot beverages. Rates are $60 single and $75 double. Family rates are available. Business travelers will enjoy the homey atmosphere.

A full breakfast is served in the dining room. High tea is served in the living room, and evening cordials are offered in the den.

From I-20, take exit 51 onto US 441/129. After you pass the Madison-Morgan Cultural Center, look for a Baptist church on the right and its parking lot on the left. Turn left immediately onto Central Avenue. The inn is on the next corner at Old Post Road and Central Avenue.

Turn of the Century
Victorian Bed & Breakfast

Ed and Jean Hancock
450 Pine Street
Madison, GA 30650
706-342-1890

$65-$75 • Open all year • 3 rooms • Home stay
• No kids, no pets, no smoking, no credit cards
• Rating: 3½

In 1890, this majestic house was built in the two-over-two Piedmont style. Tasteful additions blend perfectly, resulting in the rambling house that exists today. Located on a shady knoll in Madison's historic district, the house is surrounded by sweeping lawns and ancient oak and pecan trees. Typical Queen Anne Victorian characteristics include gingerbread, shingled gables, and a wraparound porch. Willow furniture, rockers, and a porch swing entice you outdoors. The interior is meticulously restored in period antiques. The downstairs guest room has a double bed, an armoire, and a private bath. Upstairs, two spacious bedrooms share a large bath. Both rooms feature ceiling fans and decorative fireplaces. You'll find fresh flowers and fleecy robes in your room.

A full country breakfast is served in the formal dining room or on the porch. Morgan County is a dry county, but you're more than welcome to bring your own alcoholic beverages.

From I-20, take exit 51 onto US 441/129. Turn right onto Johnson Street immediately after you pass the Madison-Morgan Cultural Center. Johnson dead-ends onto Pine, and the inn is directly in front of you.

Mara's Tara Bed & Breakfast

Rowena Mara
330 West Greene Street
Milledgeville, GA 31061
912-453-2732

$55–$65 • Open all year • 3 rooms • Home stay
• Kids over 12, no pets, smoking, reservations
required, no credit cards • Rating: 3

This white-columned mansion epitomizes *Gone With the Wind*'s Tara, hence the name of this B&B. Located across from the old Governor's Mansion, the Sanford-Binion-Mara House, circa 1825, is one of Milledgeville's finest examples of Greek Revival architecture. You'll be able to picture yourself as Scarlett or Rhett rocking on the wraparound porch, dwarfed by the soaring columns.

Downstairs, the high-ceilinged rooms include formal and informal parlors for reading, conversation, games, and relaxing, as well as the formal dining room. An upstairs sitting room is also available for guests' use. Three spacious guest rooms have private baths, decorative fireplaces, TV, and air-conditioning. Most beds are canopy, four-poster, or half-tester. Rates are $55 single and $65 double.

Guests may choose a Continental or full southern breakfast, served in the formal dining room. Rowena serves wine and hors d'oeuvres at cocktail time.

US 441 becomes Columbia Street as you enter town. Follow US 441 until it changes to Clark Street. The B&B is at the corner of Clark and Greene.

Old Winterville Inn

Don and Julie Bower
108 South Main Street
Winterville, GA 30683
706-742-7340 or 706-742-2444

$45–$70 • Open all year • 1 suite • Home stay
• Ask about kids, no pets, no smoking, no
credit cards • Rating: 3½

The Old Winterville Inn is one of the town's oldest remaining structures. Built in the 1860s, it began life as the Hunnicut Hotel, overlooking the town square and railroad depot. It served peddlers and "drummers" (traveling salesmen) who passed through town. The hotel featured ten rooms, each with a fireplace and a private entrance. In addition, the hotel housed a restaurant and the offices of the town newspaper—the *Winterville Iceberg*.

Once the hotel closed, the property fell into disrepair until purchased by the Bower family. They restored the original board-and-batten and clapboard exterior, along with the interior hand-planed plank walls and fireplace mantels. Original heart-pine floors complement primitive period furnishings.

The Old Winterville Inn occupies a tree-shaded corner lot with expansive lawns. Although the Bowers occupy most of the structure as their home, they have returned the building to its original use by renting a suite as a B&B. The suite is attached to the main house but has its own entrance and porch. It contains a sitting room with a decorative fireplace, TV, and sofa bed; a full kitchen; and a modern bath. Perfect for two guests, the suite can accommodate four. Family rates are available.

Julie's full breakfast can be served in your suite or in the Bowers's cheerful kitchen. They will try to accommodate special dietary needs. Business travelers enjoy having this cozy home away from home. The Bowers·can provide airport and university shuttle service.

From the Athens South Bypass, go east on Lexington Road (US 78). Turn left onto Old Winterville—Athens Road. As you enter Winterville, turn right onto Main Street. The inn is at the corner of Main and Suddeth.

NEWLY OPENED

Hawthorne Heights
Jennie Sheffield
600 Carlton Avenue
Union Point, GA 30669
706-486-2515

The Crockett House
Christa and Peter Crockett
671 Madison Road (US 441)
Eatonton, GA 31204
706-485-2248

5

Magnolia Midlands

Somehow, food, festivals, and lakes spring to mind when discussing the Magnolia Midlands region. After Savannah, tiny **Dublin** has the next-largest **Saint Patrick's Day Festival** in the state. The ten-day celebration includes cooking the world's largest pot of Irish beef stew, a leprechaun contest, pancake supper, fashion shows, and musical events. Other regional festivals celebrate such diverse subjects as rattlesnakes, sweet potatoes, and turpentine. There's also a stampede rodeo.

Why Dublin for the St. Patrick's Day celebration? Many people of Scotch-Irish ancestry settled on the east bank of the Oconee River during the late 1700s. John Sawyer, a pioneer citizen of the area, named the town in honor of the capital of his homeland, Ireland. Although small, Georgia's Dublin hasn't escaped worldwide attention. Irish author James Joyce refers to it on the first page of his novel *Finnegan's Wake*.

Other Dublin attractions are mills, museums, and mounds. **Chappel's Mill**, built in 1811, is still in operation. Using an old process called dry milling, it grinds 15,000 bushels of corn a year. The **Dublin-Laurens Museum** houses historic exhibits, the works of painter Lila Moore Keen, and changing displays. **Fish Trap Cut** is a marvel of construction thought to be as much as 3,000 years old. Experts surmise that the large rectangular mound, a smaller round mound, and the canal were used as a primitive fish trap.

When it comes to foods, sweet **Vidalia** onions are world famous, as are **Claxton** fruitcakes and **Stuckey's** candy. All are produced in this region. Claxton and Stuckey's in **Eastman** have showroom/outlets where you can sample and buy their wares.

The region is a national horse training center. You can visit the **Hawkinsville Harness Horse Training Facility** and watch the pacers and trotters in training from fall until early April. The town hosts horse shows from April through October.

Other attractions near Hawkinsville include **Gooseneck Farm**, a local pecan candy company; the **Historic Opera House**; and **Taylor**, the oldest home in Pulaski County.

Jefferson Memorial Park at **Irwinville** commemorates the spot where, on May 10, 1865, Confederate President Jefferson Davis was captured. There are those who insist that the Confederacy's remaining gold treasury must be buried nearby.

79

Fitzgerald's Blue & Gray Museum houses relics from "the recent unpleasantness."

The **Martin Theater** in **Douglas** hosts performing arts throughout the year, including summer's sellout "Jukebox Saturday Night," presenting fifties and sixties music. **Gaskin Avenue**, a historic district of opulent homes, was once known as "silk stocking row."

With the exception of Vidalia and Claxton, the above towns are all in the western part of the region. Moving eastward, you'll find the **Edwin I. Hatch Nuclear Plant Visitor Center** in **Baxley**. The center's animated exhibits, films, and special effects explain nuclear power. Farthest east is **Statesboro**, home of Georgia Southern University and several historic neighborhoods. Stop by the **university museum** for a look at prehistoric remains.

Lakes such as **Lake Lindsay Grace** and **Lake Mayers** and rivers such as the **Altamaha, Oconee, Canoochee**, and **Ocmulgee** provide numerous water sports. Several state parks afford various outdoor pursuits. The region also offers several excellent golf courses.

VIP Bed & Breakfast

Henry Basedow
501 North Drive
Dublin, GA 31201
912-275-3739

$40–$45 • Open all year • 1 suite • Home stay
• No kids, no pets, no smoking, no credit cards
• Rating: 4

Located across from wooded Stubbs Park, this restored 1910 bungalow was originally in Mrs. Basedow's family. In fact, she was born in the house. Her grand-
father was a photographer and he used the present sunroom as his studio. Then
the house was out of the family for about twenty-five years. In 1986 the Basedows
were able to purchase it and spent six months renovating.

Now the house features an exquisitely furnished suite that has a private entrance, bedroom, bath with Jacuzzi, parlor, gas fireplace, TV, and sunroom.
Guests can use the front porch overlooking the park. It contains an old-fashioned
porch swing and is lush with hanging ferns. The room rate is $40 single and $45
double.

A Continental breakfast of croissants, juice, and hot beverages is served.
The Basedows welcome their guests with a glass of wine.

Stubbs Park has a barbecue grill and is perfect for a picnic. In addition it
offers tennis courts and a jogging area. Dublin's renowned Saint Patrick's Day
celebration is centered here.

From I-16, turn north at exit 14 onto US 441, which becomes Telfair Street
as you come into town. Turn left at Church Street and left at North Drive. The
B&B is in the middle of the block on the right, across from Stubbs Park.

Dodge Hill Inn

Anne Riggins
105 9th Avenue, N.E.
Eastman, GA 31023
912-374-2644

$45-$55 • Open all year • 2 rooms, 2 suites
• B&B inn • Kids over 12, ask about pets, no
smoking • Rating: 3

Dodge Hill Inn is a restored turn-of-the-century home filled with antiques that are for sale, as are the collectibles and gifts.

Guest rooms have a private bath, refrigerator, phone, and TV. The downstairs suite has a sitting room; the upstairs suite has a sitting area, full kitchen, laundry facilities, balcony, and private entrance.

A traditional southern-style full breakfast is served in the dining room. Ann changes the menu frequently for long-term guests. Rates are $45 single and $55 double. Group rates are available.

Guests are welcomed with homemade cake. Sodas are always available in the refrigerator. Eastman is the home of the famous Stuckey Candy Company, and a box of this delicious confection is placed in each guest room.

You can walk to the downtown shops and restaurants. Two historic tours of Eastman are available. Little Ocmulgee State Park, hunting, fishing, golf, horseback riding, and tennis are available nearby.

Entering town from the south via US 341/23, turn east onto Ninth Avenue. The B&B is the second house on the left.

The Black Swan Inn
Bill and Mary Jane Pace
411 Progress Avenue
Hawkinsville, GA 31036
912-783-4466

$55-$70 • Open all year • 6 rooms • Country
inn • Kids, no pets, smoking • Rating: 4

The epitome of a southern antebellum mansion, this gracious 1905 Classical
Revival home crowns a large landscaped lot. Originally built for a wealthy cotton
planter, it was opened as a B&B and restaurant in 1990.

All the traditionally furnished and decorated rooms are appointed with a
private bath, ceiling fan, and decorative fireplace as well as TV and phone. Most
rooms feature a double bed; one room has twin beds. The VIP Room offers a
whirlpool bath. Two adjoining upstairs rooms can be combined to create a suite.
In addition to the ample downstairs porch that is shared with the dining room
guests, a private upstairs porch with a swing is for inn guests only.

A Continental breakfast is served in the elegant dining room or on the
cheery porch. More elaborate southern breakfasts are available on request. The intimate restaurant serves Continental cuisine with a French flair—dinner Monday
through Saturday and lunch Monday through Wednesday.

Because no one lives at the inn, each guest has a key to the rear door and
can come and go at will.

From I-75, take exit 43 at Perry, then US 341 east. After the exit for the US
341 Bypass, the road becomes Progress Avenue. The inn is on your right. From
I-16, take the Cochran exit (exit 11) onto State 26. As you approach Hawkinsville,
the road becomes Commerce Street. Turn right onto Progress Avenue. The inn is
on the left.

The Trowell House

Yvonne and Mallard Lowell
256 East Cherry Street
Jesup, GA 31545
912-530-6611

$45–$90 • Open all year • 4 rooms, 1 suite
• Country inn • Kids over 12, no pets,
restricted smoking • Rating: 4

Built in 1902, this house is typical Queen Anne Victorian with a wraparound front porch and a tower. Winner of a Georgia Trust for Historic Preservation Citation of Excellence, the house took more than a year to rehabilitate. The corbeled brick chimneys were rebuilt and the column capitals were replicated. The project is featured in a state presentation called "Travelling Through Time: Restoring Historic Houses as Bed and Breakfast Inns."

The first floor of the inn serves as a restaurant, open daily (except Sunday) for lunch and dinner. Guest rooms are located on the second and third floors.

All guest accommodations are decorated in antiques and period reproductions. All have TV, phone, and private bath, some with a claw-foot tub. Two rooms have decorative fireplaces; the suite has an electric fireplace.

The romantic suite, occupying the entire third floor, is perfect for honeymoons, anniversaries, and other special occasions. It has a vaulted ceiling, fireplace, chandelier, stained-glass window, and wet bar. Alcoves divide the room into sleeping and sitting areas; the queen-size bed is actually in the tower. The bathroom has a double sink, separate shower, and huge Jacuzzi. You'll find fresh flowers and fruit in your room. Guests can relax on the wicker-filled front porch or in either of two courtyards.

A Continental-plus breakfast is served in the dining room. The restaurant serves lunch Monday through Friday and dinner Thursday through Saturday.

The Trowell House is located within the city limits on US 341, Cherry Street, two blocks east of downtown.

The Robert Toombs Inn

Judy Barrett and Robert Faver
101 South State Street
Lyons, GA 30436
912-526-4489

$28–$55 • Open all year • 12 rooms, 6 suites
• Country inn • Kids, no pets, smoking
• Rating: 3

Named for the Confederate secretary of state, The Robert Toombs Inn captures turn-of-the-century charm. Located in the center of town, this B&B is housed in two restored buildings that were originally built as a hotel. Part of the street level of the brick structure contains a furniture store; the remainder serves as the hotel's lobby, restaurant, and lounge. Although tiny, the charming lobby features a fireplace and comfortable sofas. The upper level contains the guest rooms. Rates are a bargain, especially for business travelers.

Guest rooms are simply furnished in traditional style and colonial reproductions. Each room has a private bath and TV. Some rooms feature decorative fireplaces, king- or queen-size beds, and ceiling fans. Rooms are named after regular guests. Each suite has a bedroom and a living room. One suite can sleep extra people on a sofa bed. The other living rooms are furnished with a sofa or love seats.

A Continental breakfast is served in the restaurant. The lounge and restaurant are open in the evenings.

The hotel is in the midst of the town's shopping district and is conveniently located for exploring Savannah, Saint Marys, and the Golden Isles.

From I-16, take US 1 south into Lyons. The hotel is on the corner in the center of town.

Statesboro Inn

Garges family
106 South Main Street
Statesboro, GA 30458
912-489-8628 or 800-489-9466

$65-$90 • Open all year • 3 rooms, 2 suites
• Country inn • Kids, no pets, restricted
smoking • Rating: 4

Built in 1905 by W. G. Raines, this elegantly restored inn is listed on the National Register of Historic Places. It is conveniently located on the major thoroughfare in Statesboro. The inn's restaurant, The Raines Room, boasts a European chef who specializes in Italian and French dishes.

Exterior architectural details of special note are a wraparound front porch, small upstairs porch, rear screened-in porch, patio, and courtyard. Inside you'll find fourteen-foot ceilings, burnished woodwork, and antique furnishings.

Guest rooms are decorated in antiques and reproductions. Each room has a private bath, ceiling fan, TV, and phone. Many are appointed with decorative fireplaces, and two have Jacuzzis. The suites each feature a whirlpool and wet bar. The inn is popular with business travelers and is suitable for small corporate meetings. Corporate rates are available.

A full breakfast is served in the dining room. The restaurant is open evenings from Tuesday through Saturday.

From I-16, turn north onto US 301/25, which runs through town. The Statesboro Inn is located on US 301 a mile north of the university.

6

Northeast Mountains

The stunning natural beauty of the **Blue Ridge** and **Appalachian Mountains** spans the seasons: winter may provide enough snow for skiing, spring is vibrant with flowering trees, summer is cool, and fall's flamboyant displays rival those in New England. Streams, waterfalls, lakes, trails, and state parks offer just about anything the nature lover could desire. The southern end of the **Appalachian Trail** is in this region. And there are golf courses and scores of tennis courts that attract sports enthusiasts.

In addition, small historic towns, endless craft and antique shops, factory outlets, restaurants, entertainment, varied and delightful accommodations, and frequent fairs and festivals lure visitors year-round. We particularly like the mountain regions because they remind us of growing up in western Maryland and western Pennsylvania. Many a transplanted northerner treks to the area for a periodic mountain "fix."

The Northeast Georgia Mountains region contains the highest peak in the state—**Brasstown Bald**, with an elevation of 4,784 feet. You can drive partway up and park near a rustic gift shop. The hale and hearty can hike the rest of the way on the steep but paved paths. Others may choose to take the frequent shuttle. No matter how you get there, the view of four states is worth the effort. The summit has a ranger station and an interpretive center that offers a short film. Rangers are on hand to answer questions.

Some of Georgia's best-known mountain towns are near Brasstown Bald. **Hiawassee** is the home of the **Georgia Mountain Fair**—an annual twelve-day August event featuring a Pioneer Village and authentic mountain craft demonstrations. **Blairsville** has several lakes, state parks, waterfalls, and archaeological sites.

You've probably heard of **Alpine Helen** (often abbreviated as simply Helen) and **Cleveland**. These towns divide the region down the middle. **Helen** was a sleepy hamlet along the Chattahoochee River that almost died when the timber industry declined. However, the town fathers transformed the town into a Bavarian village to attract tourists. The facades of old buildings and all new ones are built in the Bavarian fashion. Shops on the square and narrow cobblestone streets carry German, Irish, and Scandinavian merchandise. In restaurants you'll be served German food, beer, and wine by a wait staff dressed in Bavarian costumes.

If you yearn for more natural surroundings, you can find them in the state parks just outside Helen. At **Unicoi State Park** you can see the spectacular double waterfall called **Anna Ruby Falls**. **The Sautee-Nacoochee Indian Mound** is south of Helen.

Cleveland is the home of **Babyland General Hospital**, where Cabbage Patch Kids are born and are available for adoption. Stop by the **White County Welcome Center**, housed in an old jail.

The **Sautee** and **Nacoochee Valleys** offer restful vistas. The **Old Sautee Store** has an unusual collection of old-time merchandise. The **Stovall Covered Bridge**, built in 1895, is the smallest covered bridge in Georgia.

In the extreme northeast corner of Georgia is **Rabun County**, with several state parks, wildlife management areas, waterfalls, world-class white-water rafting on the Chattooga River, and skiing at **Sky Valley**. **Lakes Burton, Rabun,** and **Seed** offer water activities. **Tallulah Gorge**, at 1,100 feet deep, is second only to the Grand Canyon in depth. Through this gorge flow **Tempesta, Oceana,** and **Hurricane Falls**. **Tallulah Gorge Park** includes the Old Town Museum, gift shop, and nature walk. Across the street is the **Tallulah Gallery**, an art collection housed in a restored Victorian mansion. Within sight is **Terrora Park and Visitor Center**.

In the southeastern part of the region is **Habersham County** and the Victorian town of **Clarkesville**, a popular retirement community. The town square has shops and art galleries. **Moccasin Creek State Park** and **Panther Creek Falls** are easily accessible.

Georgia is rapidly developing as a wine-producing state. Several wineries are located in Northeast Georgia. **Habersham Winery** in Baldwin, **Cavender Castle** in Dahlonega, and **Chateau Elan** and **Chestnut Mountain Winery**, both near **Braselton**, feature tours, tastings, and sales.

Along the Georgia-South Carolina border are **Lakes Russell** and **Hartwell**. On the grounds of tiny Toccoa College is spectacular 186-foot **Toccoa Falls**.

Elberton's claim to fame is granite. The **Georgia Guidestones**—six gargantuan stones that appeared in a country field in 1979—were made from pyramid blue granite at the direction of an anonymous group of conservationists. The sayings, or guides, are chiseled into the nineteen-foot upright stones in twelve languages. They are brief maxims espousing population control and other conservation themes. The capstone is scored so the sun will mark the time of day and the seasons. The massive monument weighs more than 119 tons. The **Elberton Granite Museum & Exhibit** in town contains historical artifacts and educational displays.

Moving back toward the western part of the region, you come to **Dahlonega**, site of America's first gold rush. The gold that covers the State Capitol dome in Atlanta is from Dahlonega. The attractive Greek Revival **Dahlonega Courthouse**, the oldest public building in Georgia, houses the **Gold Museum**. Several locations in town offer the opportunity to pan for gold, and some mines are still in operation and open for tours. Numerous state parks and waterfalls surround the town. **Amicalola Falls**, at 729 feet, is the tallest waterfall east of the Rockies.

Lake Lanier is a 38,000-acre lake just north of Atlanta. **Lake Lanier Islands**, a 1,200-acre recreation facility, includes beaches, water sports, and a water park. **Green Street Station/Georgia Mountain Museum** in nearby Gainesville features exhibits tracing the history of the area, arts and crafts, and medical paraphernalia. The complex also houses the **Elachee Creative Museum** and the **Nature Science Center.**

Lanier Raceway offers the NASCAR-Winston Racing Series. **Road Atlanta** provides racing for sportscars, motorcycles, and carts as well as being the home of the Sports Car Club of America National Championship Race.

God's Country Farm

Arlene and Bill Gray
Route 4, Box 4380
Blairsville, GA 30512
706-745-1560

$50-$70 • Open April-October • 1 room
• Home stay • Kids, no pets, no smoking,
reservations required, no credit cards • Rating: 3

In a serene, natural setting that you could indeed describe as God's country is a fifty-acre farm offering B&B accommodations. Because the farm adjoins national forest land, it is assured a future unmarred by development. In addition to growing vegetables, fruits, and livestock, Arlene and Bill declare, "We grow peace and tranquility here." That's what the vacationers come for.

The Grays spent eight years renovating the ninety-year-old, one-and-a-half-story farmhouse. A generous front deck has bent willow furniture; an enclosed sunporch features wicker. The interior of the house radiates cozy country charm.

B&B accommodations are offered in a small twin-bedded room with a private bath. A hearty, full country breakfast is served in the dining room. The Grays have built three rustic cabins on the property, but breakfast is not included with a stay in the cabins.

Guests can just relax or they can experience a real farm vacation—assisting with the livestock or picking fresh blueberries, apples, or grapes. A one-acre bass pond adjacent to the house has fine fishing. Plenty of fishing gear is available, as are indoor and outdoor games. Arlene might even teach you the art of quilting. Television reception is poor, but you can watch videos.

In addition to the attractions of the national forest, visitors can enjoy water sports at Lake Nottely, less than a mile away.

From US 76 between Blairsville and Blue Ridge, turn north onto State 325. Go two miles to a stop sign and turn left. In just less than a mile is a prominent sign on the right identifying the farm.

Burns-Sutton House

Jo Ann Smith
124 South Washington Street
Clarkesville, GA 30523
706-754-5565

$45–$75 • Open all year • 7 rooms, 2 suites
• Country inn • Kids, no pets, no smoking
• Rating: 4

This stately 1901 asymmetrical Queen Anne Victorian mansion stands on a large shaded lot along Clarkesville's main street. The home serves both as a B&B and restaurant.

Listed on the National Register of Historic Places, the mansion features a formal interior that shows off high ceilings and varnished hardwood floors. Other original architectural gems include stained-glass windows, delicate cutwork in the balustrades, picture molding, and ornate mantels. Guests are encouraged to relax in the downstairs parlor and on the large wraparound veranda.

Each guest room is furnished with antiques. Many of the rooms have decorative fireplaces, a few with gas logs. Some rooms have private baths; others share. One suite has two bedrooms—one with a king-size bed, the other with twins. The other suite has a bedroom and a sitting room with a trundle daybed. Corporate and seasonal rates are available.

A full breakfast is served in the breakfast room. In the restaurant, lunch is served to the public daily, and dinner on Friday and Saturday.

Northeast Georgia has a wealth of attractions, from waterfalls to antique shops. Clarkesville makes a good base from which to explore.

From US 23/441, take the Clarkesville exit (State 197), which becomes Washington Street inside the city limits. The inn is on the west side of the street several blocks south of the town square.

The Charm House Inn

Fred and Mary Newman
108 South Washington Street
Clarkesville, GA 30523
706-754-9347

$75–$100 • Open all year • 5 rooms • Country
inn • Kids over 10, no pets, smoking, weekend
reservations required • Rating: 4

The Charm House Inn is an elegant 1907 Greek Revival mansion that serves both
as a B&B and a restaurant. Downstairs, in addition to the dining rooms, you'll
find a large entrance hall and two parlors, one with an antique organ. All downstairs rooms have fireplaces. The downstairs is often used for private functions.
The grand upstairs hall is arranged as a sitting room for overnight guests, with a
sofa, comfortable chairs, TV, card/game table, and an ample supply of games and
magazines. High-ceilinged guest rooms are large and airy, with antiques, ceiling
fans, and private baths. Although the inn is located on a busy street, it is set well
back on the lot, so traffic noise is minimal. The inn attracts business travelers and
is suitable for small corporate meetings.

A full breakfast is served in the dining room or on the veranda. The restaurant is open for lunch daily and for dinner Thursday through Sunday.

Guests can relax at the tables and chairs on the vast front porch, or in the
large swing in the side yard. Coffee, tea, soft drinks, and homemade cake are
always available.

From US 23/441, take the Clarkesville exit onto State 197, which becomes
Washington Street inside the city limits. The inn is on the east side of the street
several blocks south of the town square.

Glen-Ella Springs Inn and Conference Center

Barrie and Bobby Aycock
Bear Gap Road
Clarkesville, GA 30523
706-754-7295 or 800-552-3479 out of state

$80–$150 • Open all year • 14 rooms, 2 suites
• Country inn • Kids, no pets, restricted
smoking, provision for disabled, reservations
required • Rating: 5

The sight of the rambling 100-year-old Glen-Ella Springs Inn nestled among the trees with a large meadow stretching out behind it assures you that you've found the perfect setting for relaxation and rejuvenation.

The inn was built between the 1830s and 1905 by Glen and Ella Davidson—a stern, hardworking farm couple—as their home. They added a second building in 1890 to house paying guests. The popularity of the area as a summer getaway ensured the hotel's success. Barrie and Bobby Aycock purchased the inn in 1986 and renovated it in compliance with national restoration criteria, which earned them a Citation of Excellence from the Georgia Trust for Historic Preservation and a listing on the National Register of Historic Places.

The Aycocks have added a first-rate restaurant. The inn has a small conference center and is popular for seminars and business get-togethers. Corporate rates are available. A two-night minimum is required if your stay includes a Saturday.

Guest rooms are decorated with antiques and locally handcrafted pieces. Each room has a private bath and phone and opens onto a porch supplied with rocking chairs. Several rooms have whirlpool baths, TVs, and gas fireplaces. Both suites consist of a bedroom, sitting room, bath, and dressing room. The parlor, furnished with antiques and cozy chintzes, is centered around a gigantic stone fireplace.

A Continental breakfast buffet is served in the dining room. You might want to take your breakfast onto one of the porches or decks. Dinner is served in the restaurant Tuesday through Sunday.

The grounds offer seventeen acres of nature trails along Panther Creek, herb and flower gardens, a garden shop, swimming pool with spacious sundeck, and the original mineral spring that first attracted guests.

From new US 23/441, take the Clarkesville exit onto State 197 into town. Go north 8.7 miles, then follow the signs to the inn, on Bear Gap Road, which is dirt-gravel. The inn is on the left.

Habersham Hollow
Country Inn & Cabins

C. J. and Maryann Gibbons
Route 6, Box 6208
Clarkesville, GA 30523
706-754-5147

$65–$85 • Open all year • 1 room, 1 suite,
2 cabins • B&B inn • Ask about kids and small
pets, no smoking • Rating: 4

Located in a woodsy country setting at the end of a dirt road, this property is excellent for those who want to get away from it all. The house is of rustic, contemporary style, which lends itself to an informal atmosphere. It features a full-length front porch with rockers and a screened-in back porch. The guest room features a Franklin stove. Guest rooms and cabins are decorated in cozy country style, with private baths and king- or queen-size beds. The spacious suite in the main house sports a garden tub, fireplace, and private porch. The cabins (ask about rates) have a deck with grill and picnic table, a full kitchen, fireplace, ceiling fan, and loft.

A full breakfast is served beside a crackling fire in the dining room or on one of the porches, depending on the season. You'll be welcomed with a complimentary bottle of the Gibbons's privately labeled wine.

From State 75, turn east at the Indian Mound onto State 17. The entrance road to the inn is four miles east of the Old Sautee Store. Look for the signs and turn right onto Preacher Campbell Road.

Spring Hill

Laura and Dumah Harrison
Route 5
Clarkesville, GA 30523
706-754-7094

$40-$90 • Open all year • 4 rooms, 1 suite
• Home stay • Kids, no pets, no smoking,
reservations required • Rating: 3

Located in the country, this B&B is in a twenty-year-old lodge-type house on a wooded lot. Guest rooms are decorated in a mix of styles. One room features a brass bed and a private deck. Two rooms share a bath.

The suite has a separate entrance, private bath, huge great room with a TV and woodstove, and a kitchen. The bedroom has a queen-size bed and two twin beds. Rates are $40 single, $50-$75 double, and $60-$90 for the suite.

The Harrisons invite guests to relax in their great room and enjoy the fireplace, TV, books, and games. Liquor is not encouraged. Guests can use the swimming pool and water slide as well as the picnic tables. Wooded hiking trails on the property allow you to exercise and enjoy nature without getting in your car.

A full breakfast of biscuits, grits, pancakes, two meats, eggs, fruit and juice, jellies, and jams is served family style in the dining room or on the deck.

From old US 23/441, turn west on New Liberty Road. Spring Hill is the fifth house on the right.

English Manor Inns
Susan Thornwell
Highway 76
Clayton, GA 30525
706-782-5789 or 800-782-5780

$49–$198 • Open all year • 7 buildings, 39
rooms, 10 suites • B&B hotel • Kids, small pets,
smoking • Rating: 5

Our first visit to English Manor was for a mystery weekend written and produced by the property's energetic mistress, Susan Thornwell. We were so entranced, we've been back numerous times.

The inn has seven buildings sprawled across seven heavily wooded acres adjacent to the Chattahoochee National Forest. Decor ranges from antiques to comfortable country modern.

The elegant main inn began as a 1912 Sears kit house and has been enlarged several times. It now houses a great room, music room, formal living room, kitchen, dining room, and thirteen guest rooms, some with fireplaces. It has period antiques, gorgeous wallpaper, plush carpeting, elegant draperies, and elaborate bed linens.

Each of the other structures—ranging from three to seven bedrooms—features its own common room and kitchen facilities, so that a group or family can take over an entire building. All guest rooms offer private baths; some have whirlpool tubs. Each building features a porch with comfortable chairs and rockers, air-conditioning, and eclectic but comfortable furniture. A few suites offer full kitchens or kitchenettes. A hot tub and swimming pool are down by the creek. The inn attracts business travelers and is well appointed for small- to mid-sized corporate meetings. The Thornwells also offer accommodations at the St. Moritz Lodge on Lake Rabun.

A full country breakfast is served in the dining room of the main inn. Special events include mystery weekends, art classes, theme parties, and dances. Christmas and Thanksgiving celebrations are particularly popular. A two-night minimum is required for holidays, special events, and most weekends. Ask about credit cards.

From US 23/441 in Clayton, turn east onto US 76. English Manor is about one mile ahead on the right.

Green Shutters
Bed & Breakfast Inn

Steve Mazarkey
Main Street
Clayton, GA 30525
706-782-3342 or 800-535-5971

$75–$150 • Open all year • 2 rooms, 1 suite
• B&B inn • Ask about kids, no pets, restricted
smoking • Rating: 3

Steve is in his fourteenth year of owning and operating the famed Green Shutters
Restaurant, noted for its woodstove cooking. Although he has lived in Clayton all
that time, he says he didn't realize this stunning property even existed because it's
so successfully hidden. He discovered it only when looking for the perfect property
for a bed and breakfast.

After four turns off the highway, you leave civilization behind and enter
deep woods. Finally you come upon a formal brick and cast-iron gate. At the top
of the hill is an exquisite Cape Cod–style house.

Although the house is surrounded by trees, the 5,600-square-foot interior is
well lit by numerous floor-to-ceiling windows. There is a huge living room with a
fireplace, a large dining room, and three guest rooms. The master suite features a
private bath and sauna. The two guest rooms are connected by a shared bath. All
rooms have queen-size beds and cable TV.

A Continental breakfast is served in the dining room. The restaurant is
open for three meals a day from April 1 through November 30. Make Thanksgiving dinner reservations far in advance.

Check in at the Green Shutters Restaurant. From US 23/441, turn left at
the second road past the high school on the right. Turn right at the BP gas
station. The restaurant is on the left. From US 76, go two blocks and turn left
onto Main Street. The restaurant is on the right on the outskirts of town.

The Lodge at Windy Acres
Marilyn and Joe Snow
Highway 75
Cleveland, GA 30528
706-865-6635

$39–$54 • Open all year • 5 rooms • B&B inn
• No kids, no pets, restricted smoking, no
credit cards • Rating: 3

The Snows designed and built the rustic, contemporary Lodge at Windy Acres
with the comfort and needs of their guests in mind. The B&B sits on a heavily
wooded hillside between Cleveland and Helen.

Inside, a round vaulted ceiling crowns the huge antique-filled great room.
The striking room features two conversation areas, a TV, piano, and fireplace with
a woodstove insert. The separate game room is well stocked with books, games,
puzzles, and a TV. Guest rooms are simply furnished. Each has a private bath and
opens onto a deck or porch. A laundry room is available to guests. The inn is
appropriate for a small corporate meeting.

A full breakfast is served in the great room. Guests can choose from a menu
that includes two juices, three meats, two kinds of eggs, French toast or pancakes,
toast or English muffin, choice of beverage, and grits or home fries. Guests also
have kitchen privileges.

The Lodge at Windy Acres is located on State 75 between Cleveland and
Helen. When approaching from Cleveland, the inn is between mile markers 3 and
4 on the left—clearly identified by a sign.

Tyson Homestead

Mary and J. T. Tyson
Highway 75
Cleveland, GA 30528
706-865-6914

$45–$65 • Open all year • 5 rooms • Home stay
• Kids, no pets, no smoking, reservations
requested, no credit cards • Rating: 3

This ten-year-old brick colonial accented by four white columns perches on a wooded hillside overlooking a large trout-stocked pond. The tranquil atmosphere encourages quiet strolls around the property. Although located in the country on twelve wooded acres, it is just five minutes from both Cleveland and Helen.

Mr. Tyson is a retired Baptist minister and Mrs. Tyson is a retired teacher. They continue to share their interest in people by offering B&B accommodations. The furnishings of the house are an eclectic mixture of styles collected by the Tysons over many years. The guest rooms share a bath. Family rates are available.

A Continental-plus breakfast of sweet rolls, muffins, eggs, cereal, fruit, juice, and hot beverages is served in the dining room. Guests are invited to relax on the patio or down at the pond, where chairs and an umbrella table are provided. Liquor is not permitted.

On State 75 from Cleveland toward Helen, just past mile marker 3, is a small lake on the right. Turn into the next drive at the mailbox for Tyson Homestead.

The Pittman House

Tom and Dot Tomberlin
103 Homer Street
Commerce, GA 30529
706-335-3823

$45–$65 • Open all year • 4 rooms • Home stay
• Kids, no pets, no smoking, reservations
preferred • Rating: 3

The book and movie called *Cold Sassy Tree* by Olive Ann Burns was based on life in Commerce, Georgia.

Refugees from suburban Atlanta, Tom and Dot have transformed this spacious home into a peaceful haven with good conversation and scrumptious food. The house is full of antiques, and the Tomberlins run the antique and craft shop next door.

A huge white-columned front porch with a flagstone floor wraps around this 1890 house. Guests will enjoy surveying the world from the sturdy rockers or porch swing.

The enormous upstairs hall has been converted to a guest sitting room with comfortable chairs and a TV, but you're just as likely to sit around the kitchen table chatting with your hosts. Bedrooms, which boast decorative fireplaces, are furnished in antiques and radiate country charm. Two pairs of guest rooms each share a bath. Although the house is air conditioned, rooms are also equipped with ceiling fans. Rates are $45–$50 single, $50–$55 double, $65 for four adults.

The property is on a busy highway and adjacent to an even busier intersection; however, we weren't bothered by traffic noise.

A full breakfast is served in the cheery kitchen or in the formal dining room. Liquor is not permitted.

Sports enthusiasts can find golf, tennis, and fishing nearby.

From I-85, take exit 53 and go south on US 441. Turn north at Homer Street. The inn is on the left.

Cavender Castle Winery and Bed & Breakfast

Linad and Wesley Phillips
US 19/State 60
Dahlonega, GA 30533
706-864-4759 or 404-577-1111

$60–$100 • Open all year • 6 rooms • B&B inn
• Kids over 12, no pets, provision for disabled
• Rating: 3

This newly constructed Gothic-style castle/winery—surrounded by grape vines—sits atop a mountain two miles from Dahlonega's historic square. Decks and high towers offer spectacular panoramas of the North Georgia mountains as well as capturing refreshing breezes.

When we last visited, three bed and breakfast rooms were complete, one of which can be a suite. Bedding sizes vary—double, queen, and king. The small room that accompanies the suite has a twin bed. Rooms are furnished in period reproductions. Each has a private bath.

A full breakfast of cereal, assorted pastries, either eggs or French toast, and bacon or sausage is served in the wine-tasting room.

This establishment is a working winery open for public tours, tastings, and sales from Friday through Monday. The winery has won bronze medals for its wines at the Atlanta International Wine Festival and the Atlanta Wine Summit.

From the Dahlonega town square, take State 52 north. Go straight through the traffic light. Turn left onto US 19/State 60 and go about two miles. At Crisson's Gold Mine turn left and follow the signs.

Miner's Deja Vu Inn

Sally and Judy Miner
300 West Main Street
Dahlonega, GA 30533
706-864-6472

$65–$75 • Open all year • 3 rooms • Home
stay • Kids over 6, no pets, no smoking,
reservations requested • Rating: 3½

The second oldest structure in Dahlonega, this stately white house was built in 1842. A wide veranda enhances the downstairs; a smaller porch adorns the upstairs. Both are equipped with comfortable rockers, which encourage guests to admire the ancient trees and lush flowers.

The rooms are spacious and feature high ceilings typical of the era. Both public and guest rooms are exquisitely furnished with Victorian antiques. All guest rooms have private baths and decorative fireplaces. Bedding varies from double to queen- and king-size beds.

A family-style breakfast consisting of an assortment of fruit, juice, hot beverages, homemade breads and pastries, as well as a main dish that might include omelettes, eggs Benedict, or a breakfast casserole is served in the dining room. Afternoons, cookies or breads are served along with a refreshing beverage. Liqueurs are available in the evening.

The inn is on West Main Street, two blocks west of the Dahlonega town square, and is clearly identified with a sign.

Mountain Top Lodge
David Middleton
Old Ellijay Road
Dahlonega, GA 30533
706-864-5257 or 800-526-9754

$65–$125 • Open all year • 13 rooms • B&B
inn • Kids over 12, no pets, no smoking
• Rating: 4

Mountain Top Lodge is unusual among bed and breakfasts because it was built specifically to serve as a B&B. The rustic country inn perches on a mountaintop surrounded by forty acres of woods. This is a wonderful spot for those who want seclusion but still want to be close to many attractions.

The cathedral-ceilinged great room features a woodstove and two large sitting areas—one in a loft. Both accommodate guests for reading, playing games, and watching TV. The loft area features a library, piano, and game tables. A variety of guest rooms—all with private baths—are decorated in country charm. Some rooms offer queen-size beds and fireplaces; two feature Jacuzzis. There is a hot tub on the back deck. Other places to relax include the front porch or the covered patio on the lower level. Guests can prepare their own light snacks in a small hospitality kitchen.

Hillside Lodge is an additional building with four guest rooms. Mountain Top Lodge is especially well-suited for family reunions and small corporate meetings.

Breakfast menus vary but may include ham, sausage, eggs, grits, frittata, quiche, fruits, and juices. Breakfast is served in the cheerful breakfast room. Sherry is offered in the public areas. If a group takes the whole facility, dinner can be included at an additional fee.

From the Dahlonega town square, take State 52 west. Go 3.5 miles and turn right onto Siloam Road. Go half a mile and turn right onto Old Ellijay Road, which ends at the entrance to the lodge.

Royal Guard Inn

John and Farris Vanderhoff
203 South Park Street
Dahlonega, GA 30533
706-864-1713

$65–$75 • Open all year • 4 rooms, 1 suite
• Home stay • Ask about kids, no pets, no
smoking • Rating: 3

This restored turn-of-the-century house features a Scandinavian theme. Renovation and an addition make this historic home a blend of old and new.

One of the best features of the B&B is its large wraparound front porch. We arrived on a rainy day, but folks were playing cards on the porch—evidently determined to enjoy the out-of-doors despite the weather.

Furnishings are an eclectic mix of styles. The large guest rooms have private baths and TV. The Royal Suite contains a bay window from which to enjoy the view.

A full breakfast of juice, fruit, an egg and sausage casserole, muffins, Danish pastries, and hot beverages is served Scandinavian style (buffet or smorgasbord) in the dining room or on the porch. On weekends, Farris serves brunch. Guests are treated to wine and cheese in the afternoon.

The inn is one-half block south of the town square on South Park Street.

Smith House Inn

Fred and Shirley Welch
202 South Chestatee
Dahlonega, GA 30533
706-864-3566 or 800-852-9577

$40–$60 • Open all year • 16 rooms • Country
inn • Kids, no pets, restricted smoking,
provision for disabled • Rating: 4

Located just off the town square, this 1884 structure has, since 1922, operated as a mountain inn presenting hearty southern home cooking at its best—all-you-can-eat banquets served family style. The restaurant developed a following because of its fine food and southern hospitality.

Captain Hall—original owner of the land—discovered gold on it but was never permitted to mine because the vein is in the center of town, so he built his house over it. However, today you can pan for gold in the front yard.

Guest rooms are in the main house and the elegant carriage house, both of which offer comfortable sitting rooms where guests can congregate. The guest rooms—all with private bath—are decorated with coordinating fabrics and wallpaper and furnished with antique reproductions. Many feature original stained-glass windows. Modern amenities include tile baths with showers or claw-foot tubs, air-conditioning, TV, and VCR.

A wide veranda wraps around the first floor of the main house. Shaded by ancient pines and magnolias and amply furnished with comfortable rockers, the porch attracts visitors to relax. There is also a swimming pool.

A Continental breakfast is served in the sitting room of the carriage house. Diners at the Smith House are seated family style on a first-come, first-served basis. The restaurant is open for lunch and dinner Tuesday through Sunday.

From the south, the inn is on the left side of State 60 just before you reach the town square.

Worley Homestead Inn

Mary and Bill Scott
410 West Main Street
Dahlonega, GA 30533
706-864-7002

$55-$75 • Open all year • 7 rooms • B&B inn
• No kids, no pets, no smoking • Rating: 4

What is now the circular driveway in front of the two-story inn was once the old road to Atlanta. For a long time in its history, the inn housed cadets from North Georgia College.

Today the atmosphere of the Worley Homestead is that of a very upscale stagecoach stop. The 1842 Victorian house is in mint condition. Without the high ceilings so typical of the period, the house has a very cozy feel. Furnishings are exquisite antiques—some reminiscent of farm trappings, others more formal, such as those in the parlor.

Guest rooms are decorated in antiques. All rooms have cable TV and a private bath. We were fascinated by the working antique toilet with a tin-lined water reservoir in one of the baths. Some guest rooms have decorative fireplaces.

Worley Homestead is popular with business travelers. The whole house can be rented for family reunions or small corporate meetings.

A hearty full breakfast, consisting of juice, fruit, meat, grits, breads, and a choice of two main dishes that run the gamut from quiche to blueberry crepes to omelettes, is served in the dining room.

Guests can enjoy the downstairs and upstairs front porches, the flagstone patio, or the gazebo in the sunken backyard.

The inn is located on the right side of State 52 west about four blocks from the town square and across from North Georgia College.

Grenoke Bed & Breakfast

Wright P. Cousins
914 Elbert Extension
Elberton, GA 30635
706-283-1567

$50–$60 • Open all year • 4 rooms • Home stay
• Ask about kids, no pets, restricted smoking
• Rating: 3

Grenoke is a lovely red brick Georgian home in an ancestral setting. An immense lawn sweeps back from the busy highway to the stately house, almost hidden from view by the avenue of elms. Once you reach the house, you'd never know a bustling, modern world existed out there.

The property was the home of Nancy Hart, colonial spy and heroine of the American Revolution.

Comfortable guest rooms offer private or shared baths. Grenoke is very popular with business travelers.

Wright, who often does catering, serves a full breakfast featuring one of her specialties, such as an egg casserole or creamed turkey on toast. Guests are encouraged to use the refrigerator.

From I-85, take exit 58 onto State 17 south toward Elberton. Just past the center of town, watch for Grenoke's sign on the right.

Rainbow Manor

Joyce and Al Florence
217 Heard Street
Elberton, GA 30635
706-213-0314

$50–$60 • Open all year • 5 rooms • Country
inn • Kids, no pets, restricted smoking
• Rating: 3

A large porch supported by massive columns was added to the original 1882 house, giving the Rainbow Manor a Greek Revival appearance. What were once parlor and dining room now contain a restaurant. Part of the front yard and all of the side yard have been paved to provide parking—somewhat taking away from the elegant appearance.

A spacious downstairs bedroom has a private bath and sitting area. The room's focal point is a four-poster bed with a knotted canopy. In addition, the room has a decorative fireplace, ceiling fan, and TV.

Joyce has embellished the stairway to the second floor with floral stencils on the risers. The large upstairs hall is a comfortable sitting room for guests. Each set of two bedrooms is connected by a shared bath. Guest rooms are furnished in antiques. Each has a decorative fireplace, ceiling fan, air-conditioning, and TV. Two rooms have double beds and one contains twin beds. Because three rooms provide a desk, many business people stay at Rainbow Manor. Rates are $50 single, $60 double. Ask about family rates.

Both light and hearty breakfasts are served in the restaurant. B&B guests are served evening desserts.

From State 72, turn south onto State 77 and go one block. Traffic is one way around the town square. As you complete the third side, exit onto Heard Street. After the traffic light, the inn is the third house on the left.

Whitworth Inn

Ken and Chris Jonick
6593 McEver Road
Flowery Branch, GA 30542
706-967-2386

$55 • Open all year • 9 rooms • B&B inn
• Kids, no pets, restricted smoking, provision
for disabled • Rating: 3

Set back from the highway on a wooded lot, the Whitworth Inn resembles an elegant oversized home with full-length porches on both the first and second floors.

The only public rooms are the dining room and a sitting room that contains comfortable seating, a TV, and a selection of books and magazines. Visitors can also enjoy the porches and backyard gazebo. Guest rooms have private baths and ceiling fans. Most beds are queen-size, although a few are doubles or twins. Rates are per room for one or two guests. A third person in the room is an additional $10. Inquire about special rates for extended stays. The inn features meeting space that can be used for conferences or catered parties. It is ideal for small corporate gatherings and is a popular place for parties and wedding receptions.

A full breakfast is served in the dining room or on the patio. Juice and baked goods are left out for guest snacks.

Activities on nearby Lake Lanier are the most popular reason for staying at the Whitworth Inn. These include sailing, boating, golf, beaches, water parks, concerts, and picnicking. The Chateau Elan Winery and Golf Course as well as Road Atlanta are nearby.

From I-985 north of Atlanta, take exit 2 to Flowery Branch. Turn west off the exit ramp, proceed one mile to the stop sign, turn left on State 13, and go one block to the first right turn. Go one-quarter mile to the blinking light and turn right onto McEver Road. The inn is 1.9 miles ahead on the right.

Dunlap House

Ann and Ben Ventress
635 Green Street
Gainesville, GA 30501
404-536-0200 or 800-462-6992

$85–$125 • Open all year • 10 rooms • B&B
inn • Kids, no pets, no smoking, provision for
disabled • Rating: 4

The elegance of the Old South is epitomized in this gracious house. Located in a historic Gainesville neighborhood, Dunlap House has hosted such notables as Paul Newman and Tom Cruise.

Luxurious guest rooms have private baths and king- or queen-size beds. Each room offers a telephone and a built-in remote-control cable TV. The accommodations are enhanced with designer linens, oversized cotton bath towels, and plush terry robes. Some rooms are appointed with fireplaces.

An ample Continental breakfast of fresh fruit, juice, cereal, muffins, and hot beverages is served. You can choose to eat in your room, in the common room, or on the porch.

Refreshments are served on arrival, and tea, coffee, and light snacks are always available. Nightly turn-down service includes a mint on your pillow. Each room is provided with bottled water. Evening tea is served in fall.

From either I-85 (exit 50) or I-985 (exit 6), proceed west on US 129. In Gainesville the road becomes Butler Parkway, which merges with Green Street. Dunlap House is on the left on the corner of Ridgewood and Green.

Dutch Cottage

Bill and Jane Vander Werf
Ridge Road
Helen, GA 30545
706-878-3135

$50-$65 • Open May-October • 4 rooms,
1 cabin • Home stay • Kids, no pets, smoking,
no credit cards • Rating: 3

Dutch Cottage is a rustic house perched on a woody hillside above Helen. In homage to the Vander Werf's Dutch background, the cottage is furnished and generously decorated with of blue and white, ceramics, wooden shoes, and other memorabilia.

Accommodations are either in the main house or in a cabin behind the house. Rooms are named for Jane's sisters. Dena—the most striking room— features a Dutch wall bed fashioned from a cedar chest. Some rooms have private baths; others share. The cabin sleeps four. You'll feel like you're sitting in a tree house if you make use of the large patio overlooking the woods.

A Continental-plus breakfast buffet is served in the dining room. It might consist of a breakfast casserole or French toast with accompaniments.

The Vander Werfs can shuttle you back and forth to the shops, restaurants, and other attractions of Helen in their 1930 Ford.

From State 17/75 in Helen, turn west at the Presbyterian church onto Hamby Street. After you cross a bridge, turn right. Go one block and take the left fork up the hill. A discreet sign identifies the inn.

Hilltop Haus

Melissa Dean
Chattahoochee Street
Helen, GA 30545
706-878-2388

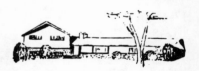

$45–$75 • Open all year • 4 rooms, 1 efficiency
• Home stay • Kids, no pets, no smoking,
provision for disabled • Rating: 3

This is a contemporary split-level lodge located on a hilltop overlooking Helen and the Chattahoochee River. Guest rooms with private baths are in the main part of the house. The three-room efficiency with its own entrance is located in the walk-out basement. The efficiency can accommodate up to four guests. Furnishings are simple. Fresh flowers enhance the guest rooms.

A full country breakfast including bacon, eggs, coffee cake, juice, fruit, and hot beverages is served. A homemade dessert is offered at check-in.

The house is within walking distance of Helen's shops, outlets, restaurants, and other attractions. But remember—it's all uphill on the way back.

From State 17/75 in Helen, turn east in front of City Hall. Go one-quarter mile around a sharp bend. Hilltop Haus is at the end of the street.

Grahl's Comfort Zone

Shirley and Darwin Grahl
River Street
Hiawassee, GA 30546
706-896-1358

$60 • Open all year • 2 rooms • Home stay
• Kids, no pets, no smoking • Rating: 3

The Grahls offer B&B accommodations in their newly constructed home on the shore of Lake Chatuge. Though the house is deceptively small from the outside, the rooms are large and light filled. Walls of windows overlook the ever-changing scenery and activities of the lake. Contemporary furnishings foster an informal atmosphere.

Guest rooms have private baths. For traveling families, extra guests can be accommodated on the sofa bed in the downstairs sitting room, and cots can be provided. With the lake just outside your door, you can lounge on the decks, the patio, the terraced lawn, or on the dock. In chilly weather, you can curl up by the fireplace in the downstairs sitting room. Because the Grahls are musically inclined, music is piped throughout the house, and they encourage guests to join them for sing-alongs at the grand piano. Cable TV, plentiful books, and magazines provide relaxation.

Shirley serves a full breakfast in the dining room using her formal china, silver, and crystal. The meal might include fruit, juice, muffins, a breakfast meat, and an egg dish. It always includes her special fried potatoes.

The lake itself is the main attraction. Boating, fishing, and other water sports are available at nearby marinas.

From US 76 in the center of Hiawassee, at the blinking light turn south on River Street. In the second block, you'll pass the courthouse on the left. The B&B is located in the right side of the cream-colored duplex, also on the left.

Swan Lake B&B
Linda and Ray Elam
2500 Hickorynut Cove
Hiawassee, GA 30546
706-896-1582

$60–$75 • Open January-November • 2 rooms
• Home stay • Kids, no pets, no smoking,
reservations required, no credit cards • Rating: 4

When the Elams built their stunning contemporary version of a Cape Cod house overlooking Swan Lake, they created the lower level to accommodate guests. Both the house and lake are located on the grounds of their business—the Hickory Nut Trout Farm and Campground—but are completely hidden from view. The get-away-from-it-all feeling is enhanced by the fact that the property is adjacent to national forest and wilderness areas. The Elams consider their property "a heaven for people—a haven for nature."

The guest level contains a common sitting room and two guest rooms. Walls of windows in all three rooms overlook the lake (which is home to a pair of swans), with majestic Eagle Mountain as the backdrop. The guest rooms have private baths, walk-in closets, queen-size beds, daybeds, ceiling fans, and TVs. Each room opens onto the patio with old-fashioned porch swings. Rates are per couple; additional guests over ten years old are an extra $10. Ask about corporate and family rates.

Linda serves a full breakfast in the dining room, or you may eat it in your room or on the porch.

The guest sitting room has a fireplace, game area, TV, stereo, and a microwave and refrigerator. In the late afternoon, Linda prepares a surprise refreshment such as banana splits or her special Swan Lake Splash.

You can use the inn's fishing boat and gear, the paddleboat, or bicycles. Paths surround the lake, and you can hike up into the national forest. Ask about guided hiking tours, four-wheel drive-tours, and white-water rafting.

From US 76 in Hiawassee, take State 75 north. Go about two miles to Upper Bell Road and turn right. Go about four miles to a sign for Hickory Nut Trout Farm on the right. Turn right and follow the signs to the trout farm office.

Lake Rabun Hotel

William Petties
P.O. Box 10
Lakemont, GA 30552
706-782-4946

$54.50 • Open all year • 16 rooms • B&B inn
• Kids, no pets, no smoking • Rating: 3

Across the road from Lake Rabun is a rustic mountain inn that is family oriented, relaxed, friendly, and comfortable. The landmark was built in 1922 from dark wood and Georgia stone. Planters and stone seats jut from the stone foundations and chimneys. Shade trees surround the inn without spoiling the view. Guests can enjoy the lattice-covered stone patio.

Inside the walls are paneled, the floors are uncovered except for some braided rugs, and the furniture is simple. Many pieces are fashioned from rhododendron and mountain laurel branches. The great room has a large stone fireplace and a good supply of games, books, and magazines. Guest rooms are small and spartan, although each features ruffled tieback curtains and new country bedspreads or colorful quilts as well as new area rugs. There are nine bathrooms for the sixteen guest rooms. The honeymoon bedroom features a corner fireplace. There is a minimum two-night stay on weekends. The entire hotel can be reserved for $800 per night.

This is the type of hotel that was appealing to your grandparents. Today, it's for those who like simplicity and informality. It would be a good site for a corporate gathering or family reunion. Swimming, boating, and fishing are available right across the street.

A Continental breakfast of bagels, muffins, fruit, juice, coffee, and tea is served.

From US 441/23 north, turn left at the Lakemont/Lake Rabun sign two miles north of Tallulah Falls. Proceed two miles and turn left at Lakemont Building Supply onto Lake Rabun Road. The hotel is two miles ahead on the right. From US 441/23 south, turn right at the convenience store and Clayton Carpet Center. Make a sharp left and proceed four miles to the hotel.

The York House

Tim and Kimberlee Cook
P.O. Box 126
Mountain City, GA 30562
706-746-2068 or 800-231-9675

$55-$70 • Open all year • 12 rooms, 1 suite
• B&B inn • Kids, no pets, restricted smoking,
provision for disabled • Rating: 3½

Although an original structure was built before 1850, the building that remains today was built in 1896 as an inn. At that time it was so popular with folks who wanted to get away to the cool mountains in summer that it had its own railroad station. Its long-gone dance hall had the first piano in Rabun County. Listed on the National Register of Historic Places, the inn is nestled in a valley among the mountains between Clayton and Dillard.

Just as it was originally, the inn is furnished plainly and simply. In fact, some of the original iron beds remain. Guest rooms are carpeted and contain a bed, armoire, dresser, and straight chair. Each has a private bath and a separate entrance onto one of the porches. The honeymoon suite features its own fireplace. Downstairs are two matching parlors with fireplaces at either end. Guests are encouraged to gather here to watch cable TV, read, mingle, and relax. The property also has two streams, trails, and picnic areas. Equipment is available for volleyball and shuffleboard.

A Continental-plus breakfast of juices and assorted pastries can be brought to your room on a silver tray, or you can enjoy it on one of the porches.

Take US 441/23 north from Clayton to Mountain City. Turn right at the sign for the inn which is one-quarter mile ahead on the right.

Grandpa's Room
Mack and Lib Tucker
Highway 17
Nacoochee-Sautee, GA 30571
706-878-2364

$25–$30 per person • Open all year • 3 rooms
• Home stay • Kids, no pets, restricted
smoking, reservations required • Rating: 3

This 1872 Victorian farmhouse was built by Lib's great-grandfather. The family stopped farming long ago, so although the house is located in the country, it is surrounded by gigantic trees rather than by working fields. Built as a private residence, it took in boarders in the early 1900s, just as it is doing today.

The dwelling is rustic and strewn with all the memorabilia a family would amass in more than 120 years in the same house. The atmosphere is friendly and very informal.

Each guest room is decorated in farm-style antiques. Rooms contain two double beds, a TV, and a ceiling fan. The fact that the house isn't air conditioned is of little concern in the cool mountains. In fact, the fireplace in the parlor gets more use than an air conditioner ever would. Both floors of the house feature large porches filled with comfortable rockers.

Whereas most B&Bs charge by the room, this one charges by the person. Adults are $25–$30 each, children twelve to eighteen are half price, and children under twelve are free when they share a room with their parents. Cribs are $5 extra.

A full country breakfast of fruit, grits, sausage, biscuits, and jellies is served. An attached shop features antiques and mountain crafts. The attraction of the Nacoochee and Sautee Valleys are nearby, as is the well-known Sautee General Store.

From State 75 just south of Helen, turn right onto State 17 at the Indian Mound. The B&B is two miles ahead on the left, just past the Old Sautee Store.

The Lumsden Homeplace
Mike and Linda Crittenden
Guy Palmer Road
Sautee, GA 30571
706-878-2813

$65 • Open all year • 5 rooms • Home stay
• Kids over 12, no pets, no smoking,
reservations requested, no credit cards
• Rating: 3

Lumsden Homeplace is an 1890 mountain farmhouse that was built by Mike's great-grandfather—a Civil War veteran, gold miner, farmer, and state senator. The Crittendens did the restoration themselves, including rewiring and upgrading the plumbing and electrical systems, which earned them a Georgia Trust for Historic Preservation Citation of Excellence.

The house is furnished with family antiques. You can see Mike and Linda's love and pride in every detail, such as the floral wallpapers and pastel colors. Although the house has several fireplaces, the only one in use is in the parlor, where guests are encouraged to use the ample supply of books.

Each guest room has a private bath and is furnished with family heirlooms and period antiques. You can expect iron beds, antique quilts, wicker, floral prints, and dhurrie rugs.

The three-story house sits on a knoll with an expansive yard in the front and thick woods in the back. In spring and summer, the yard bursts with wild and cultivated flowers planted years ago by Mike's aunts. Visitors can enjoy the tranquil view from either the downstairs or upstairs porches, which are filled with rocking chairs, plants, a swing, and a hammock. If you like hiking or bird-watching, you can explore the woods behind the house.

Breakfast features such delights as fresh ginger custard, cheese biscuits, ham or poached eggs with bacon, or cornmeal pancakes. It is served in the sunny breakfast nook off the parlor.

From State 75 south of Helen, turn east onto State 17 at the Indian Mound. At the Old Sautee Store, turn north onto State 255. Immediately past the Community Center on the left and the Presbyterian church on the right, Guy Palmer Road angles off to the right. Watch closely; the road sign is hard to see. The inn is the first home you come to.

Nacoochee Valley Guest House

Bernadette Yates
State Highway 17
Sautee, GA 30571
706-878-3830

$65–$95 • Open all year • 4 rooms • Country inn • Kids, pets, no smoking, provision for disabled • Rating: 3½

Although this charming B&B is modest on the outside, you'll be delighted with the interior, and with its energetic owner, Bernadette. The house, built in the 1920s, overlooks the scenic Nacoochee Valley. In addition to serving as a B&B, Nacoochee Valley Guest House has a superb restaurant and bake shop. The house features antique furnishings and a working fireplace in the living room.

Guest rooms all have private baths. The Honeymoon Suite contains a king-size bed and a fireplace. The Oak Room has a queen-size bed, a private entrance, and a bay window with a spectacular valley view. All guests can enjoy the view of the valley from the rear deck. Family rates are available.

Bernadette serves a full breakfast in the breakfast room. It might include such dishes as omelettes, quiche, eggs, popovers, griddle cakes, meat, muffins, fresh fruit, juice, and granola along with European coffee. Bernadette also serves afternoon tea with cakes and tarts. Guests are encouraged to use the barbecue grill and picnic table. You must make dinner reservations for the elegant restaurant. Guests who stay two nights are presented with a bottle of private-label wine.

The inn is located on State 17 east of Helen at the entrance to the Sautee Valley.

The Stovall House

Ham Schwartz
State Highway 255
Sautee, GA 30571
706-878-3355

$40–$70 • Open all year • 5 rooms • Country
inn • Kids, ask about pets, smoking restricted,
provision for disabled • Rating: 4

Set in the tranquil Sautee Valley near Helen, this restored 1837 farmhouse was
built by Moses Harshaw, a colorful character reputed to be "the meanest man who
ever lived." Now serving as a B&B as well as an award-winning restaurant, the
house is named after the William Stovall family, who lived in it from 1839 to the
1940s. The house is on the National Register of Historic Places and has won
awards from the Georgia Trust for Historic Preservation and the Georgia Mountain Area Planning and Development Corporation. *Georgia Trend* has listed the
restaurant as one of the fifty best in the state.

   One guest room is located on the first floor; the rest are upstairs. All guest
rooms have a private bath. Skylights in the upstairs hall and each upstairs guest
room make the rooms light and airy. A sleeping porch can be combined with two
guest rooms to create a large suite. Cribs and rollaways are available. Some rooms
have working fireplaces. Family, group, and extended-stay rates are available.

   Guests can enjoy the 360-degree valley and mountain views from rocking
chairs on the ample verandas. Guests are also invited to use the parlor, stocked
with games, puzzles, books, and magazines.

   A Continental-plus breakfast of muffins, fruit, juice, and hot beverages is
served in the dining room. The restaurant serves dinner Tuesday through Sunday,
lunch Tuesday through Saturday, and Sunday brunch.

   From State 75 between Cleveland and Helen, take State 17 east at the
Indian Mound. At the Old Sautee Store, turn north onto State 255. The inn is
on the right at about mile marker 13 and is clearly identified by a sign.

Woodhaven Chalet
Ginger Wunderlich
Covered Bridge Road
Sautee, GA 30571
706-878-2580

$55–$65 • Open all year • 2 rooms, 1 suite
• Home stay • Kids over 12, no pets, restricted
smoking, no credit cards • Rating: 3

Hidden away in the Sautee Valley is comfortable Woodhaven Chalet. Of contemporary design, the rustic house is surrounded by deep woods and wildflower gardens. Eclectic furnishings accentuate the informal atmosphere. Blending into the hillside, the house occupies three levels. The uppermost level contains two guest rooms furnished in antiques and country crafts; the rooms share a bath.

The suite occupies the lowest level. The large great room includes a sleeping area, queen-size sofa bed, sitting area with TV and fireplace, dining area, and full kitchen. This level offers a private entrance, patio, barbecue grill, and an old-fashioned swing. Guests are encouraged to use the ground-level great room and its stone fireplace, the music loft, the decks, and porches. Join the Wunderlichs in a sing-along at the grand piano.

Ginger serves a Continental-plus breakfast. Guests may choose to eat in the formal dining room using china, crystal, and silver, or opt to be more informal on the sunporch. Sherry is available in the afternoon.

From State 75 just south of Helen, turn east onto State 17 at the Indian Mound. Turn left onto State 255 at the Sautee Store. Immediately after mile marker 15, turn left onto Covered Bridge Road. Woodhaven Chalet is the second house on the right.

Habersham Manor House

Ken and Gail Davis
326 West Doyle Street
Toccoa, GA 30577
706-886-6496

$47.50–$60 • Open all year • 3 rooms • Home
stay • Kids, no pets, restricted smoking
• Rating: 3½

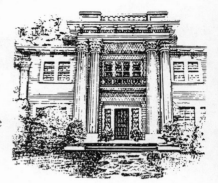

Habersham Manor—the epitome of a 1906 Greek Revival mansion dominated by huge white columns—sits on a small lot in the center of town. Although the Davises are a relatively young couple, they have traveled and lived all over the world and are glad to share experiences with their guests.

Previous owners restored the maple floors and rosewood moldings and redecorated the house with period reproduction wallpapers and paints. The exquisite furnishings and draperies remain. A central hall is flanked by two magnificent parlors, each with an impressive fireplace. One parlor is for smokers and one for nonsmokers. The second-floor hallway has been converted into another, more casual sitting area for guests. The guest rooms have twin or double four-poster beds, private or shared baths, and comfortable seating; some rooms have a desk and/or gas fireplace. A deck with comfortable furniture overlooks a garden and fish pond at the rear of the house.

A full breakfast is served, which might include eggs Benedict or omelettes, three types of homemade bread and rolls, fruit, juice, and coffee or tea. On request, you can luxuriate with breakfast in bed. Beverages and fresh home-baked cookies are always available.

Habersham Manor House is located two blocks west of Stephens County Courthouse Square, just off State 17.

Simmons-Bond Inn

Laura and Marvin Ross
130 West Tugalo Avenue
Toccoa, GA 30577
706-886-8411 or 800-706-7677

$40–$59 • Open all year • 5 rooms • Country
inn • Kids over 12, small pets, no smoking
• Rating: 3½

An excellent example of asymmetric Victorian architecture, this restored 1903 home is on the National Register of Historic Places. Now a restaurant and B&B, the house is located on a large corner lot opposite the town square and Stephens County Courthouse.

Interior architectural highlights include beveled glass, burnished oak woodwork, and elaborately carved fireplaces. A semicircular alcove is accented by stained-glass windows. The great hall and dining room feature oak pilasters and Ionic columns. Three rooms still boast their original chandeliers and wall lamps. Victorian furnishings grace the rooms.

Because the downstairs is devoted to the restaurant and pub, comfortable seating for guests is limited to their rooms or the large wraparound porch, overflowing with hanging ferns. The guest rooms have decorative fireplaces, ceiling fans, cable TV, telephone, and king- or queen-size beds. This B&B is popular with business travelers. Corporate (as well as family) rates are available.

A full breakfast is served in the dining room. The restaurant has a beer and wine license and serves lunch and dinner weeknights. The inn is popular for wedding receptions and parties.

From the north on US 23/441, exit south onto State 17, then follow State 184 south into Toccoa. From the south on I-85, take exit 58 onto State 17 and go north to State 184. The inn is on the courthouse square.

NEWLY OPENED

Beechwood Inn
Marty Loft
P.O. Box 120
Clayton, GA 30525
706-782-5094

The Blackberry Patch
Robert and Bobbie Jean Havlish
P.O. Box 601
Mountain City, GA 30562
706-746-5632

Habersham House
Stan Wilbanks
Route 4, Box 4066
Clarkesville, GA 30523
706-754-4767

Lake Front Suite
Stella and Vernie Burleson
P.O. Box 647
Hiawassee, GA 30546
706-896-1331

Mountain Memories
Yolanda Keating
385 Chancey Drive
Hiawassee, GA 30546
800-335-8439

Souther Country Inn
Georgia Citrin
2592 Collins Lane
Blairsville, GA 30512
706-379-3095

Staunton Storehouse
Diana Stodart-Mason
202 North Meaders Street
Dahlonega, GA 30533
706-864-6114

Valley of Hidden Paths
Sissa Bethea
Route 1, Box 410
Rabun Gap, GA 30568
706-746-2278
Northwest Mountains

7
Northwest Mountains

Considered almost inseparable is a ten-mile region straddling the Georgia-Tennessee state borders that includes extreme Northwest Georgia—**Chickamauga, Fort Oglethorpe,** and **Lookout Mountain**—and Chattanooga, Tennessee. Not only were the areas inexorably linked by a series of decisive Civil War battles, but today some of the world-famous attractions associated with Chattanooga, such as Rock City Gardens, actually lie across the border in Georgia.

If you're interested in Civil War history, we suggest that you begin with the **Chickamauga/Chattanooga National Military Park** in North Georgia and Tennessee as well as the **Confederama** in Chattanooga. Together they'll give you an excellent overview of the connection between the battles and their far-reaching consequences.

Chickamauga was the site of one of the Confederacy's greatest victories. The Georgia battlefield park has a new ultramodern and comprehensive visitors center with a film describing the battle. Exhibits include the **Fuller Gun Collection**—one of the most extensive anywhere of Civil War guns.

The Chattanooga end of the park includes **Point Park,** overlooking the river, and a visitor center. The nearby **Cravens House Museum**, the only structure remaining from the Civil War era, is furnished with period pieces and features tours by costumed guides.

The **Confederama**, located in a small castlelike building in Chattanooga, is a miniature model of the Chattanooga area, with 5,000 toy soldiers and 650 lights. During the narrative, different areas are spotlighted, and sound effects add to the reality.

Other attractions on the Tennessee side include the **Lookout Mountain Incline Railway, Ruby Falls,** the **Tennessee Valley Railroad**, and the **TVA Energy Center**.

Back in Georgia, **Barnsley Gardens** near **Adairsville** reflects the romance of the antebellum period. Thirty acres of English-style gardens have been restored: a grand boxwood parterre garden with a twelve-foot fountain, a small boxwood garden with antique roses, bog and water gardens, fernery, rockery, woodland gardens, and an orchard. One intact wing of the house serves as a museum. A garden center sells heirloom and antique roses, perennials, trees, and shrubs.

Two major trails offer a systematic way to tour this region. The **Chieftains Trail** stresses Indian heritage; the **Blue Gray Trail** concentrates on the Civil War.

A significant stop on the Chieftains Trail is the **Etowah Indian Mounds State Historic Site** near **Cartersville**. The flat-topped earthen knolls—the highest of which is sixty-three feet—were used between A.D. 1000 and 1500 as platforms for temples, mortuaries, and homes of priest-chiefs. Nobility were buried in the mounds, dressed in elaborate costumes and accompanied by personal items they would need in their afterlives. Stairways allow you to climb the mounds without harming the steeply sloping sides. From the top you get a 360-degree panorama of the Etowah Valley. The interpretive center of this National Historic Landmark contains artifacts, life-size figures, paintings, and historical explanations.

Elsewhere on the trail, you can visit **Chief Vann's House** in **Chatsworth** and the **Major John Ridge House** in **Rome**. Ridge was a Cherokee chief, and his house contains the **Chieftains Museum**. In **Tate**, you'll find remains of the Cherokee **Old Harnage Tavern**. **Fort Mountain** may have been an Indian ceremonial center.

The Blue Gray Trail stretches 130 miles from Chickamauga to **Marietta**, a suburb of Atlanta. Explore the **Big Shanty Museum** in Adairsville and the **Kennesaw Mountain National Battlefield Park** at Kennesaw.

Near **Dallas** is the **Pickett's Mill Historic Site**, the location of an important Southern victory. Still containing Civil War fortifications, the battlefield is considered to be one of the best kept in the nation. It offers a video, exhibits, and hiking trails.

Other important sites on the trail are the **Blunt House** in **Dalton** and the **Gordon-Lee Mansion** (now a B&B) in **Chickamauga**. Significant battles were fought at **Resaca** and **Ringgold**. The battle of Resaca is reenacted each year. On Marietta's **Cannonball Trail** you can see antebellum homes that survived the Battle of Atlanta.

Working north to south, you'll find many attractions of this region that aren't on either of the trails. **Cloudland Canyon**—in the extreme northwest corner of the state—is a natural wonder. The history of the carpet industry is told at **Crown Gardens and Archives** in Dalton. Visit **Calhoun**'s **Mercer Air Museum**, an outdoor collection of historic planes. **Oakleigh**—once Sherman's headquarters—houses the Gordon County Historical Society.

Rome was so named because it has three rivers and seven hills. The **Martha Berry Museum** features historic artifacts, artworks, formal gardens, nature trails, and an old mill. The historic downtown includes a restored Victorian river district.

Near **Cartersville**, in addition to the Etowah Indian Mounds, see **Air Acres Museum**, an outdoor collection of historic planes; the **Cassville Confederate Cemetery**; **Cooper's Iron Works**; **Etowah Arts Gallery**; **Etowah Historical Museum**; historic downtown; **Lowery Covered Bridge**, the oldest in Georgia; **Noble Hill**, a black history museum and cultural center; **Roselawn**

Museum, home of famous evangelist Sam P. Jones; and the **Weinman Mineral Center and Museum**. **Lake Allatoona** offers varied water activities, as does **Lake Arrowhead**.

Cave Spring was so named because of the large limestone cave whose spring supplied water to the community. A city park has sprung up around the cave, which is open for tours. The town of Cave Spring is well known for its antique shops.

At the extreme northeastern corner of the region, **Ellijay** is the apple capital of Georgia and attracts visitors to its many antique shops. **Carter's Lake** and **Blue Ridge Lake** are nearby. **Tate** is the world's largest producer of marble. You can tour the **Georgia Marble Company** and the mines during the Marble Festival in October. is an old stone-grind, water-driven mill still in use today. **John's Mill** is an old stone-grind, water-driven mill still in use today.

Old Home Place

Joan and Vince Mayer
764 Union Grove Church Road, S.E.
Adairsville, GA 30103
706-625-3649

$40 • Open March-Thanksgiving • 3 rooms
• Home stay • Kids over 6, pets, no smoking,
reservations required, no credit cards
• Rating: 3

The Old Home Place is aptly named. A circa 1855 country home, it is located on six serene wooded acres—all that remain from the original 4,000-acre farm. The house looks deceptively small from the outside, but once inside you'll find spacious rooms with nineteen-foot ceilings. The decor is simple and the furnishings are antiques. Most rooms have decorative fireplaces. All guest rooms share a single bath. Each guest room offers a double and a twin bed. Family rates are available.

A cozy wing has been added onto the original house. This is where the Mayers live and where the Continental breakfast is served. The Mayers encourage guests to use the great room.

From I-75, turn onto State 53 at exit 129. Go east to Union Grove Church Road and turn right. It is 1.3 miles to the inn, which is on the left at a sharp curve in the road.

The Bowdon Inn

Diana and Jackie Jackson
130 West College Street
Bowdon, GA 30109
404-258-5469 or 404-258-9808

$42 • Open all year • 2 rooms • Home stay
• Kids, ask about pets, smoking, no credit cards
• Rating: 4

Winner of a Chamber of Commerce Beautification Award, this 1877 Queen Anne
Victorian is tiny Bowden's crown jewel. Beautifully restored, the house is painted
in shades of gray accented with white and brick-red trim and has a large wraparound porch. A generous supply of rockers offer guests complete relaxation.

The interior has heart-pine floors, beaded wainscoting, and beaded and parquet ceilings. Two guest rooms are separated by a comfortable shared sitting room
with TV, stereo, books, and magazines.

Guest rooms are decorated in period reproductions and wallpapers. One
room has twin brass beds; the other has a double bed. Both have a decorative fireplace, ceiling fan, and private bath with claw-foot tub. The double room has a private entrance onto the porch.

A full or Continental breakfast is served in the dining room.

A fully restored antebellum cottage on the property contains a gift shop and
Bowden Area Historical Society items. The inn hosts numerous weddings, receptions, and luncheons. A friendly ghost, described as a "cranky eccentric," occupies the house. The Jacksons delight in regaling guests with the ghost's antics.

From I-20, take exit 1 (State 100) south for about 9.5 miles. At the traffic
light in the center of town, turn right. The house is about one block ahead on the
right, clearly identified by a large sign.

Stoneleigh

Jim Lay
316 Fain Street
Calhoun, GA 30701
706-629-2093

$45–$60 • Open April–December • 2 rooms,
1 suite • Home stay • Kids, no pets, restricted
smoking, provision for disabled, reservations
required, no credit cards • Rating: 3½

Jim Lay is your cheerful and fascinating host at Stoneleigh—the 1901 Craftsman-style home that has always been in his family. The house is decorated in family antiques and memorabilia collected by Jim and his relatives during a century of world travel.

The formal sitting room is bathed in sunshine and furnished in antiques. The ceiling is ornamented by center and corner plaster medallions.

Guests may choose from the first-floor suite with private bath or one of the two upstairs rooms that share a bath. The suite has a sunny bedroom with a mantle from a house Sherman nearly destroyed and the cannonball high-poster bed in which Jim was born. It also features a small sitting room/library with a fireplace. Family rates are available.

A full hunt breakfast chosen from a menu is served on china in the formal dining room or more casually outside on the patio. A typical breakfast might include juice, cereal, eggs, meat, grits, and homemade breads.

Jim will offer you sherry and cookies on arrival. You'll also find fresh flowers, candy, and fruit in your room. The chaise lounge and other comfortable lawn chairs will draw you to relax in the enclosed backyard. But best of all, Jim entertains you with tales of local and family history, ghost stories, and his experiences in the Peace Corps.

From I-75, take exit 130 west onto State 156. Go 2.3 miles beyond the Holiday Inn and turn left onto College Avenue, then left onto Fain Street. The house is in the middle of the block.

Hearn Academy Inn

Joyce Goddard
Box 715
Cave Spring, GA 30124
706-777-8865

$50-$60 • Open spring-fall • 5 rooms • B&B
inn • Kids over 12, no pets, no smoking, no
credit cards • Rating: 3

Built in 1839, this B&B—listed on the National Register of Historic Places—was
the former dormitory for the Hearn Manual Labor School, which once trained the
underprivileged. The schoolhouse still stands just across the way. Hearn Academy,
owned and operated by the Cave Spring Historical Society, is located on the
grounds of the twenty-acre city park. The spring for which the town is named is
situated in a cave, which is open for tours. The spring pumps 3 to 4 million gallons
of water a day, some of which is used to fill a 1.5-acre swimming pool shaped like
the state of Georgia. Also on the property is a Baptist church built by slaves in
1849.

The inn's interior construction as well as the furnishings and decor are simple, as would be appropriate to a school dormitory. Downstairs are four small dining rooms, a sitting room with a TV, and a large, closed-in porch where many
guests choose to eat their breakfast. One of the guest rooms has a private bath; the
other two pairs each share a bath. Guests can enjoy the rockers on the front
porch.

Business travelers find the inn homey and comfortable. It is suitable for a
small corporate meeting or small family reunion. Catering can be arranged for additional meals and/or groups.

A Continental breakfast of juice, fruit, cereal, homemade breads, and hot
beverages is served buffet style. Sherry is always available in the sitting room.

Guests will enjoy the many antique and craft shops in Cave Spring, as well
as the Doll House and the Kudzu Pottery Farm.

As you enter Cave Spring, you'll pass the town square and commercial
buildings on the right; then you'll see the entrance to the city park on the left.
Once you're in the park, the inn is on the left.

Gordon-Lee Mansion

Richard Barclift
217 Cove Road
Chickamauga, GA 30707
706-375-4728 or 800-487-4728

$65–$90 • Open all year • 3 rooms, 1 suite,
1 cabin • B&B inn • Kids over 12, no pets,
no smoking • Rating: 4½

The elegant Gordon-Lee Mansion, built in 1847, is the only structure left standing from the fierce battle of Chickamauga, where the South achieved one of its major victories during the Civil War. Built by wealthy mill owner James Gordon, the house was commandeered as a headquarters for Union Gen. William Rosencrans. One of his staff was future president James Garfield. The downstairs library was used as an operating room. Both the beauty of the structure and its historical significance qualified the house to be listed on the National Register of Historic Places.

Sitting well back from the street, the mansion is just visible through a tree-lined avenue of ancient oaks and maples. Lovingly restored and exquisitely furnished with Oriental rugs, crystal and brass chandeliers, and Federal, Empire, and early Victorian antiques, the Greek Revival house serves not only as a bed and breakfast but also as a museum. One upstairs bedroom has been converted to display Civil War memorabilia, which guests can peruse at any time.

Primary accommodations are in three luxurious bedrooms and one suite in the main house. Each has a private bath. Accommodations in the cabin are more utilitarian and more suitable for a long-term stay, perhaps by a business traveler.

A Continental-plus breakfast is served in the formal dining room. Guests are welcomed with wine and cheese.

From I-75, take exit 141 onto State 2 to Fort Oglethorpe, then go south on US 27 toward Chickamauga. Proceed all the way through the park. At the first traffic light after exiting the park, turn right. At the next traffic light turn left and follow that road until you reach the traffic light in downtown Chickamauga. Turn left again. The mansion is the fourth building on the right.

Captain's Quarters
Bed & Breakfast Inn

Pam Humphrey and Ann Gilbert
13 Barnhardt Circle
Fort Oglethorpe, GA 30742
706-858-0624

$55–$85 • Open all year • 5 rooms, 1 suite
• B&B inn • Ask about kids, no pets, no
smoking • Rating: 4

Barnhardt Circle was once the site of the officers' homes when Fort Oglethorpe was an active military facility. This is a gracious street of stately white duplex houses built around the turn of the century. Sisters Pam Humphrey and Ann Gilbert have put one of these duplexes to creative use. They live in one half and operate a B&B in the other half. The sisters also cater luncheons, teas, dinners, and bridal showers in one of the two dining rooms.

The B&B, located directly across the street from the Chickamauga National Battlefield, is elegantly furnished and fastidiously decorated. Most of the guest rooms are appointed with a king-size bed, ceiling fan, clock radio, and TV. All offer private baths—two with claw-foot tubs, the remainder with marble showers. Two rooms have decorative fireplaces. The ample porches are furnished with wicker, and flowers burst from planters in season. Business travelers, especially women, like to stay here.

A full breakfast of fruit, juice, eggs, meat, homemade breads, and tea or coffee is served in the dining room. There is a snack room with a refrigerator, sofa, table and chairs, phone, games, and magazines. An ironing board and iron are available on request.

Turn west off I-75 onto State 2. Turn left at US 27, also known as Lafayette Road. Turn right at Harker Road and left again into Barnhardt Circle.

Chanticleer Inn

Gloria Horton
1300 Mockingbird Lane
Lookout Mountain, GA 30750
706-820-2015

$35–$85 • Open all year • 16 units • B&B inn
• Kids, no pets, smoking • Rating: 3½

This charming stone motel was built in the 1930s within sight of renowned Rock City. Although most people consider the famous rock formation and gardens to be in Chattanooga, Tennessee, the tourist attraction is actually in Georgia.

Whereas most motels from the thirties are no longer appealing, this one has aged well. Several buildings sprawl across the shaded grounds.

Rooms and furnishings are typical of a motel. However, the suites feature fireplaces. There is a swimming pool and playground.

A Continental-plus breakfast of pastries, juice, and hot beverages is served in the building housing the registration desk.

From the motel, you can walk to the world-famous Rock City Gardens. On the Georgia side of the border, you should visit the Chickamauga National Battlefield. Nearby on the Tennessee side are Ruby Falls, the Confederama, Point Park, and the Incline.

Follow the signs to Rock City. Take Tennessee State 58 up Lookout Mountain from its junction with Broad Street (US 41/11/64/72). State 58 changes to State 157. Continue to the top of the mountain and turn left on Mockingbird Lane. The inn is on the corner.

Maloof Building B&B Suites

Ferris and Ann Maloof
P.O. Box 970
McCaysville, GA 30555
706-492-2016

$65–$125 • Open all year • 3 suites • B&B inn
• No kids, no pets, no smoking, reservations
required • Rating: 3

We award this B&B high marks for an excellent adaptation of a commercial building into an elegant lodging facility. Ferris Maloof's father immigrated from Lebanon in 1911 and settled in this town, which straddles the Georgia-Tennessee border; the state line is actually down the middle of the main street. On the Georgia side, the town is known as McCaysville; on the Tennessee side it is called Copperhill because of the extensive copper mining that was done here at the turn of the century. In 1921 Nassir Maloof erected the building to house his department store and living quarters for his family. Recently renovated, the historic building now houses a mall of small shops on the lower level and the B&B suites on the upper level.

Each suite has a living room with a sofa bed, private bath, full kitchen, air-conditioning, and a ceiling fan. Decor ranges from Southwest to Art Deco to cozy country charm. Ask about corporate rates.

Breakfast can be Continental or full. The kitchen is stocked with such items as homemade breads and jams, cereals, milk, yogurt, juice, and fixings for hot beverages for guests to eat in their suite at their leisure. On request, you'll be provided with vouchers for a complimentary breakfast at a local downtown restaurant.

You'll find a basket of fruit in your suite. Those celebrating a honeymoon, an anniversary, or other special occasion will find a surprise. Television isn't offered, and there's one phone in the hall for common use. Parking is on the street. The Maloofs also own the Eagle Adventure Company, which offers fishing, horseback riding, llama trekking, and white-water rafting.

From Atlanta, take I-75 north to I-575, which ends at State 5. Continue north on State 5, which goes right into McCaysville. The B&B is located in the middle of the block just past the three-way stop.

Tate House

Jeanette Calhoun
P.O. Box 33
Tate, GA 30177
404-735-3122 or 800-342-7515 in state

$115–$126 • Open all year • 5 rooms • Country
inn/resort • Kids, no pets, restricted smoking
• Rating: 5

Also known as the Pink Marble Mansion, this gorgeous home was built in 1926 by
Georgia Marble Company president Sam Tate. The rare pink Etowah marble is
found only in the vicinity of the tiny town of Tate. Inside, the house features
marble floors, baths, and fireplaces.

The house on the twenty-seven acre estate was restored in 1973, when a
restaurant, pub, cabins, and sports facilities were added. Listed on the National
Register of Historic Places, the mansion is furnished in antiques and reproductions.

The sumptuous guest rooms have private baths, king-size beds, cable TV,
and phones. The Jewel Room, which was the family's upstairs sitting room, offers
a sofa, conference table, china cupboard, desk, and an enormous bathroom. Miss
Flora's Room has a sitting area, desk, and game table. Sports facilities include a
hot tub, heated pool, two tennis courts, a jogging trail, horseback riding, and
shuffleboard. This resort is ideal for corporate retreats.

Champagne and coffee will be in your room on arrival. Room service is
available, and a valet is on night duty.

On weekdays a Continental breakfast is served; on weekends you'll be
served a full country breakfast in the main dining room. The restaurant is divided
into five dining rooms. One is very formal; another is decorated in a Southwest
motif. The Garden Room overlooks the swimming pool, marble fountains, and
statuary.

Generally, the pub and restaurant are open Wednesday through Saturday.
The restaurant serves both lunch and dinner; brunch is served on Sunday. A
dance band performs in the pub on Saturday night.

From Atlanta, take I-75 north to I-575. Continue north to State 108 and
turn right (the road becomes State 53). The inn is on the right near the junction
of State 5.

Twin Oaks

Carol and Earl Turner
9565 East Liberty Road
Villa Rica, GA 30180
404-459-4374

$85 • Open all year • 1 cottage • Home
stay/guest house • Kids, pets, smoking,
provision for disabled, reservations required,
no credit cards • Rating: 4½

Those who want a serene, private atmosphere can find just that at Twin Oaks. The exquisite guest house sits on a twenty-three-acre farm down a dirt road five minutes off I-20. The Turners built the elegant cottage well away from their house to ensure privacy. This B&B is so attractive and romantic, we think it's ideal for a honeymoon or an anniversary.

The cottage is actually one large, airy room. Sun streams through the large windows, and the reflections bounce off an entire wall of floor-to-ceiling mirrors. The cottage features twelve-foot ceilings, ceiling fans, a carpeted bedroom with queen-size bed, a kitchen and dining area, and a sitting area with a sofa bed, TV, stereo, and wood stove. A sunroom, furnished with rattan, invites guests to enjoy the view. There's also a patio and hot tub.

Guests are welcome to use the Turner's swimming pool. Fishing is available on the property. City folks will particularly enjoy the Turner's menagerie, which includes koi and goldfish in the pond, swans, ostriches, mallards, Chinese and Egyptian geese, turkeys, rabbits, chickens, dogs, and cats roaming around.

You may have a Continental or full breakfast brought to the cottage or served in the Turner's cheery kitchen.

From I-20 west of Atlanta, take exit 6 to Villa Rica. Turn left. At the second dirt road, turn left onto East Liberty. The B&B is the second driveway on the left.

NEWLY OPENED

Chandler Arms B&B
Rosemary Chandler
Rome, GA 30161
800-438-9492

Claremont House
Patsy Priest
906 East Second Avenue
Rome, GA 30161
706-291-0900 or 800-254-4797

Dalton-Holly Tree House
Dalton, GA 30720
706-278-6009

Victorian Parlour B&B
Jan White
Cloudland, GA 30731
706-862-2870

8

Plantation Trace

We were surprised to learn that during the late nineteenth century, the area of rolling red clay hills of Southwest Georgia was a magnet drawing well-to-do visitors from all over the world who came to enjoy the mild winter climate. Many built "cottages" that we'd consider mansions. However, tourists are fickle, and soon some other spot was the favored place to go. But the region didn't curl up and die. Most of its unspoiled charms remain for current travelers to discover.

The region is designated by the state as the Plantation Trace because it contains America's largest enduring collection of working plantations; at last count there were seventy-eight. Unfortunately most of them aren't open for tours. A few are open each year for pilgrimages and special events. However, you should explore **Pebble Hill Plantation**—the most magnificent and publicly accessible.

Established in 1820, the plantation was later purchased by a wealthy family to use as a winter home and hunting retreat. The original mansion was destroyed by fire in the 1930s; however, the majority of its treasures were rescued. The mansion was rebuilt by noted architect Abraham Garfield, son of President Garfield.

The last heir, Elisabeth Ireland Poe, left funds for the plantation to be opened to the public. She was an avid collector, and the house is filled with everything from Indian relics to fine porcelains. We particularly enjoyed her collection of horse-related art—from paintings to porcelains to sculpture. As fascinating as a tour of the house is, be sure to allow time for a leisurely stroll around the grounds to examine all the outbuildings.

Thomasville is the area's most significant city. Known as the City of Roses, it is the home of the **Rose Test Garden**—one of twenty-five official rose test gardens in the United States. If you visit the garden, you'll be surprised at how small it is, but you'll be overwhelmed by the beautiful experimental roses. A small shop offers roses and other plants for sale. One of the South's premier spring events is Thomasville's **Rose Show and Festival**.

While in Thomasville, visit the seven official historic districts, as well as several significant homes and churches open for tours. The 1885 **Lapham-Patterson House** was the first of the "winter" cottages. Also see the **Thomasville Cultural Center**, the **Thomas County Historical Museum**, and the **Big Oak**—a magnificent specimen that dates from 1685.

Albany is the home of the **Chehaw Wild Animal Park**, designed by famed naturalist Jim Fowler. Elevated walkways and protected trails permit visitors to see native and exotic wild animals in natural settings. Historic **Radium Springs** is considered one of Georgia's seven natural wonders.

Some of the finest quail hunting in the South is in the Plantation Trace area. **Moultrie** boasts an **Old County Jail** that resembles a Victorian resort. The **Colquitt County Arts Center** features varying exhibits. The **Sunbelt Expo**—a large agricultural exposition—is held near Moultrie each October. Nearby **Sylvester** is the home of **Peter Pan Peanut Butter**, where you can take a picture of the nine-foot carved peanut.

The **Georgia Agrirama** is located just off I-75 near **Tifton**. One of the state's most popular attractions, this is a living history center where you can learn about farm life in the late 1800s. Costumed artisans demonstrate skills that were necessary on the farm. The complex includes restored homes, shops, a school, and a church. Special events are held throughout the year.

In **Valdosta**, visit the **Crescent**—a magnificent neoclassical home that boasts gardens, a chapel, and a schoolhouse. **Barber House** is the home of the Chamber of Commerce.

One of the most fascinating attractions in this region is the **Kolomoki State Historic Park**, between Blakely and Fort Gaines. This is an important archaeological site dating to A.D. 800. The 1,300-acre park contains seven mounds built by the Swift and Weeden Indians in the twelfth and thirteenth centuries. The temple mound is one of the largest east of the Mississippi and the oldest in Georgia. The interpretive center is outstanding. You can walk into the partially excavated mound and see original artifacts in place. Replicas of the skeletal remains found there have been placed in the original positions.

The Plantation Trace contains several significant lakes, among them **Lake Walter F. George**, **Lake George W. Andrews**, and **Lake Seminole**, which offer all the water-oriented activities your heart could desire. **Lake Seminole** is rated as the fifth-best bass-fishing lake in the nation.

Layside Bed & Breakfast
Jeanine Lay
611 River Street
Blakely, GA 31723
912-723-8932

$30–$38 • Open all year • 2 rooms • Home stay
• Kids over 10, no pets, no smoking, no credit
cards • Rating: 3

Built at the turn of the century, this eighteen-room Victorian home sits in a large yard well back from the street at the head of a circular driveway. A sixty-foot front porch invites guests to enjoy leisurely afternoons.

The public areas and guest rooms are eclectically furnished. The pair of guest rooms share a bath; if only one room is rented, you'll have a private bath.

A Continental-plus breakfast is served in the dining room. It might include cereal, juice, homemade muffins, and hot beverages.

The living room is amply supplied with books, magazines, and games. The upstairs hall also serves as a sitting room for guests. Rollaway beds are available at an additional cost.

A public tennis court and swimming pool are nearby. Don't miss the Kolomoki Indian Mounds National Park, between Blakely and Fort Gaines.

From the square in Blakely, exit onto College Street, in the northeast corner of the square near a Tru-Valu Hardware store. Continue on College and across the railroad tracks. When the street dead-ends into River Street, turn right into Layside's driveway.

The Davis House

Mary Davis
64 McArthur Drive
Camilla, GA 31730
912-336-8439

$30–$45 • Open all year • 3 rooms • Home stay
• Kids, no pets, smoking, reservations required,
no credit cards • Rating: 3

Located in a quiet, pine tree–filled neighborhood, the Davis House is a traditional one-story brick residence built twenty-five years ago.

Guest accommodations are either in two rooms that share a bath with a shower or in a room with a private bath. This bed and breakfast is probably most appealing for a long-term business stay or for someone who is relocating. Inquire about family or long-term rates. Additional guests in the same room are charged $10 extra.

A simple Continental breakfast of juice, fruit, and muffins or bread—all fresh and homemade—is served in the dining area. You can request a full breakfast for only $1 extra. Guests are welcome to use the kitchen.

Golf and swimming are available at a nearby country club. Fishermen will want to try their luck on the Flint River. Riverview Plantation and Coveyrise Plantation offer quail hunting.

From US 19 in Camilla, turn east onto Broad Street, then right onto McArthur Drive. The Davis House is on the left and has a circular driveway.

Hummingbird's Perch

Frances Wilson
Route 1, Box 1870
Chula, GA 31733
912-382-5431

$40–$60 • Open all year • 3 rooms • Home
stay • Kids over 12, no pets, no smoking,
reservations required, provision for disabled
• Rating: 3½

A few years ago the Wilsons built their dream house in the country on twenty acres overlooking a seven-acre lake. When they noticed the profusion of hummingbirds, they named the property for the amazing little creatures. Vast flower gardens and numerous feeders assure that you'll get to watch the colorful living hovercrafts as much as you want.

Hummingbird's Perch is a place to get away from it all, to unwind while you enjoy the views and the peace and quiet—but with all the modern conveniences. You'll probably be greeted by one of the receptionist cats—Callie, Misty, or Twerk.

The heart of the Cape Cod-style house is a paneled family room with a cathedral ceiling and a large fireplace. An inviting sunroom opens off this room. Guests naturally congregate here in chilly weather. On warm days, it's hard to choose between the long rocking chair-filled front porch or the pleasant back patio.

The house is furnished in appropriate period reproductions. The first-floor guest room has a private bath; the two upstairs rooms share a bath. Rooms have full or queen-size beds. One room can accommodate a third person, for $10 extra. Inquire about corporate rates.

Both Continental or full breakfasts are offered. You can choose to eat in the formal dining room, kitchen, or sunroom, or on the patio, front porch, or deck.

The lake is stocked with bass, bluegill, catfish, and crappie. You can fish from the shore or dock, or take out the rowboat. On the other hand, maybe you'd rather just think about fishing from the old-fashioned swing at the water's edge.

From I-75, take exit 23—six miles north of Tifton—and go east about a mile to the first paved cross street. Turn right. The B&B is on the right.

217 Huckaby
Meg and Bond Anderson
P.O. Box 115
Parrot, GA 31777
912-623-5545

$65-$85 • Open all year • 2 rooms • Home stay
• No kids, no pets, no smoking, no credit cards
• Rating: 3

Parrott is a surprising little town in Southwest Georgia between Albany and Columbus. And we do mean little (population 220). Driving by on State 520, it you blink you'll miss it. However, if you get off the highway to explore, you'll find a sampler of turn-of-the-century architecture that ranges from cottages to mansions.

One of the more modest houses was built in 1915 as a wedding present for Meg's grandparents. It was out of the family for many years, but in 1981 the Andersons bought it and are slowly restoring it themselves. They have a ways to go yet, so you'll probably see partially finished projects and building materials.

Bond is a flutist and musical instrument designer. Meg is an artist specializing in jewelry, metalsmithing, and landscape design. Both are ardent organic gardeners. Their lifestyle is simple—back to the basics and back to nature. The B&B furnishings are plain and sparse. Both guest rooms have private baths, but the bath for one of the rooms is down the hall.

A hearty breakfast is included with the room. Other meals are available on request at an additional charge. Meals include homemade breads, international cuisine, and products from this certified organic homestead.

The Andersons offer private instruction is silversmithing, herb growing and drying, dairy goat husbandry, cheesemaking, and organic gardening.

From the State 520 Loop of State 55, turn east onto Main Street. Turn left on Leverrett Street, which dead-ends into Huckaby. Turn left. The B&B is the first house on the right.

White Columns
Ellen West
1403 West Screven Street
Quitman, GA 31643
912-263-4445

$65-$75 • Open all year • 3 rooms • Home stay
• Kids over 14, no pets, no smoking • Rating: 3

Although built in 1965, this lovely home on the outskirts of Quitman was constructed in the traditional southern plantation style. The two-story white brick
house features impressive columns across the front. It sits well back from the street
on a manicured four-acre lot dotted with huge shade trees.

The interior is decorated with an eclectic but tasteful variety of furnishings
that the Wests accumulated over the years. Guests are invited to use the large,
comfortable family room with TV, abundantly stocked bookcases, and raised fireplace. The room overlooks the patio and pool, which guests are welcome to use.

A sweeping curved staircase leads to the guest rooms on the second floor.
Two of the rooms have canopy beds and share a bath. The other guest room has
twin beds and a private bath.

A full breakfast is served in the dining room or on the patio. Breakfast
might include a fruit plate, eggs, grits or hash browns, juice, bacon or sausage,
croissants, and blueberry muffins.

Quitman claims one of the largest turn-of-the-century historic districts in
the nation. You can pick up a brochure for the driving tour at the Chamber of
Commerce. Hunting and fishing are popular diversions.

From I-75 in Valdosta, take US 84/221 west ten miles to Quitman. Go
straight through the central commercial district, then start looking for the inn's
mailbox on the right. There is no sign identifying the residence as a B&B.

1884 Paxton House

Susie Sherrod
445 Remington Avenue
Thomasville, GA 31792
912-226-5197 or 800-278-0138

$75–$120 • Open all year • 6 rooms/suites
• Home stay • Kids, no pets, restricted
smoking, reservations required • Rating: 4½

"Our aim is to pamper," says Susie Sherrod, owner of this exquisitely restored and furnished Victorian house-museum built in 1884. Her philosophy is to provide European-style service combined with southern hospitality.

When Thomasville was a fashionable winter retreat for wealthy northerners, Colonel Paxton built one of the first seasonal "cottages." To the original Victorian Gothic house, a massive neoclassical wraparound porch was added in 1905. Today this porch invites guests to relax in the numerous rockers and swings.

This gorgeous B&B is graced with twelve fireplaces, a circular staircase, twelve- to thirteen-foot ceilings, heart-pine floors, original light fixtures, beveled glass, plaster moldings, and unique transom windows. After restoring the house, Susie added custom decorating, antiques, homemade quilts, and prominent displays of her collectibles from around the world.

Each guest suite features an ornamental fireplace and a private bath. The Blue Suite has double beds, a TV, and VCR. The Eighteenth Century Suite offers a queen-size bed in one room and two twins in the other. The spacious Peach Suite is a large room with a queen-size rice bed and a sitting area, a second bedroom with twin beds, and a bathroom with a claw-foot tub with shower. Additional accommodations are located in a Victorian cottage that has been moved to the property. Inquire about corporate and family rates, as well as midweek and special occasion packages.

Susie serves an elegant gourmet breakfast on fine china, crystal, and silver. Breakfast might consist of orange-stuffed French toast, Belgian waffles, eggs Benedict, egg and cheese strata, or crepes accompanied by homemade breads, apricot jam, fresh fruits, and juices.

Fresh flowers from Susie's garden fill the house. Guests are treated to bedside chocolates, turn-down service, and refreshments in the butler's pantry. Honeymooners can expect additional pampering.

From the north on US 319, which becomes Jackson Street, turn right onto Hansell Street. The mansion is located on the corner of Remington and Hansell.

Deer Creek Bed and Breakfast

Gladys Muggeridge
1304 South Broad Street
Thomasville, GA 31792
912-226-7294

$46–$115 • Open all year • 2 rooms, 1 suite
• Home stay • Kids, no pets, no smoking, no
credit cards • Rating: 3

Deer Creek, the Muggeridge home, is named for the deer occasionally seen in the adjacent woods. The contemporary house is located on a shady two-acre lot next to the South's second-oldest country club. Views of the gardens, woods, and gurgling stream can be seen from the huge rear windows, large deck, and brick patio.

The large, eclectically furnished great room features a gas fireplace and cathedral ceiling as well as a TV, books, magazines, and games. Guest rooms are furnished in brass and antiques. Two guest rooms share a bath; the master suite has a private bath. A crib and a sofa bed are available for additional guests. Rates are $46 single and $48 double for guest rooms and $20 more for the master suite. Inquire about family and long-term rates.

Gladys serves a full breakfast. The night before, guests can choose from a menu of three types of coffee, juice, eggs, bacon, waffles, cereal, nut bread, or toast. You can have breakfast in bed, in the dining room, or in the great room. Honeymooners always get their first breakfast in bed.

Guests are encouraged to use the game table and the exercise equipment, and the screened, wicker- and wrought iron-filled indoor/outdoor room created from a carport.

From the north on US 19, take the last exit west to Thomasville (Old Monticello Road). Go two miles. Deer Creek is the first house on the left past the Glen Erven Country Club. From the east on US 84, take US 19 south. The Old Monticello Road exit is about two miles ahead.

Evans House Bed and Breakfast

Lee Puskar
725 South Hansell Street
Thomasville, GA 31792
912-226-1343 or 800-344-9717

$60–$125 • Open all year • 4 rooms • B&B inn
• Kids, no pets, no smoking, no credit cards
• Rating: 4½

For abundant southern hospitality, we recommend staying at the Evans House Bed and Breakfast. Located in Thomasville's Parkfront Historical District, directly across from twenty-seven-acre Paradise Park, this restored 1898 Victorian house with a wraparound porch is within walking distance of most of the city's attractions.

Operated by energetic Lee Puskar, the Evans House features four guest rooms with king- or queen-size beds and all with private bath. Several rooms can be combined with a library, parlor, or sitting room to create a suite. Furnishings are turn-of-the-century antiques combined with Lee's contemporary favorites.

The ample wicker-filled porches invite guests to relax in good weather. There's plenty of paved parking behind the house. Business travelers love the pampering they get at the Evans House. Corporate rates are available.

Guests are awakened to coffee or tea served in their bedroom, followed by a full gourmet breakfast in the kitchen. Lee changes the menu for guests staying more than one night.

In our investigations of more than 300 B&Bs, Lee is undoubtedly one of the best hostesses we found. Pampering her guests is her all-important credo. Tea and cookies are served on check-in, brandy and sweets at bedtime. She'll make dinner reservations for you as well as recommendations for tours. Bicycles are available on a first-come, first-served basis.

From US 319, turn onto Hansell Street, which makes a sweeping semicircle with two outlets on US 319. The Evans House is locate at Park Avenue and Hansell Street across from Paradise Park.

The Grand Victoria Inn

Anne Dodge
817 South Hansell Street
Thomasville, GA 31792
912-226-7460

$55–$70 • Open all year • 4 rooms • Home stay
• Kids, no pets, no smoking, reservations
required, no credit cards • Rating: 4½

Built in 1893, this majestic Victorian with the requisite turret and huge wrap-around porch is located across the street from twenty-seven-acre Paradise Park. Anne's painstaking restoration has earned the house a Landmark Award from the city. The mansion is surrounded by manicured lawns and a formal garden with a brick courtyard in the back where weddings and other parties are sometimes held.

Inside are ripped-pine floors, high ceilings, a huge foyer, and a unique key-hole stained-glass window. Most of the windows are original. The dining room boasts a Waterford chandelier; the room can accommodate a grand piano and still seat twenty-six. The family room, kitchen, and informal eating area are walled with burnished paneling.

Guest accommodations are on the second floor. The romantic Mrs. Keefer Room, popular with honeymooners, boasts a brass queen-size bed, wicker chaise, Jacuzzi, and gas fireplace. The Jenny Lind and Hoosier Rooms share a hall bath with a claw-foot tub. The elegant Jenny Lind Room offers a wicker queen-size bed and a seating area in a window alcove as well as a gas fireplace. The Hoosier Room sports more informal pine furniture. The Sheridan Room has a private screened porch with a hammock and glider. All have quality designer bed linens and extra-thick Egyptian cotton towels dried in the fresh air. Inquire about corporate and family rates.

An elegant gourmet breakfast is generally served in the formal dining room using linens, Limoges china, silver, and crystal. Breakfast can also be served on the porch. Picnic basket lunches are available.

Two challenging eighteen-hole golf courses are nearby. The fourth week in April is Rose Show Week (make reservations early).

From the east on US 319, turn left onto Hansell Street. The inn is on the left between Smith Avenue and Old Monticello Road.

Our Cottage on the Park

Constance and Kenneth Clineman
801 South Hansell Street
Thomasville, GA 31792
912-227-0404

$50–$80 • Open all year • 2 rooms/suites
• Home stay • Kids, no pets, no smoking,
no credit cards • Rating: 4

At the end of the nineteenth century, many wealthy northerners flocked to Thomasville for its warm climate. Because it was the end of the railroad, Thomasville was as far south as they could reach easily. Other travelers came for health reasons. It was believed that being around pine trees cured consumption.

This stately Victorian mansion was built in 1893 as a winter "cottage" for George S. Cox of Pullman Railroad Coaches. It sits in a prime location overlooking Paradise Park. Constructed of yellow heart pine with stained glass and a wraparound porch, the house is on the National Register of Historic Places and has been honored with an award by Thomasville Landmarks.

The interior is a comfortable mix of turn-of-the-century elegance and modern convenience. Furniture includes antiques and period reproductions. Guests are encouraged to use the large formal living room or the cozy informal parlor, which offers a TV, VCR, and piano.

The romantic, airy Park View Room occupies the tower and is furnished in wicker and brass. It features a decorative fireplace, and its private bath with shower is located down the hall. The Magnolia Room has an attached private bath. Both rooms have queen-size beds and ceiling fans. A small single room can be combined with either of the others to create a suite. Rooms boast luxurious robes. Junior beds and cradles are available on request. Rates are $50 single and $60 double in one guest room. Add $20 for a two-room suite.

A full breakfast is usually served in the formal dining room, although you may request to dine on one of the porches.

Our Cottage is a prime place from which to view the Rose Parade and other activities associated with the annual Rose Festival, but be sure to make reservations early.

From US 319, turn onto Hansell Street, which makes a sweeping semicircle with two outlets on US 319. Our Cottage is located at Park Avenue and Hansell Street across from Paradise Park.

Susina Plantation Inn
Anne-Marie Walker
Route 3, Box 1010
Thomasville, GA 31792
912-377-9644

$125-$175 • Open all year • 8 rooms • Country
inn • Kids, ask about pets, no smoking, no
credit cards • Rating: 5

Susina Plantation Inn is one of only two B&Bs in Georgia that we think fulfills
the stereotype of traditional southern elegance of the antebellum period. Originally called Cedar Grove, the Greek Revival plantation house was built in 1841.
Massive oaks frame the pillared front; the grounds are dotted with pecan and walnut trees.

The interior features high ceilings, gleaming woodwork, intricate carvings,
and ornate plasterwork. Antiques fill both the public rooms and guest rooms. The
various-sized accommodations are appointed with decorative fireplaces and private baths, most with claw-foot tubs. Several rooms have a private veranda or
screened-in porch. The inn is an ideal spot for a family reunion or small corporate
retreat.

Ms. Walker, a professional chef, serves a full breakfast of ham, eggs, grits,
bacon, sausage, homemade breads, and muffins. Included in the room rate is a
five-course gourmet dinner served on bone china in the formal dining room. Rates
are $125 single and $175 double, including dinner.

At Susina Plantation Inn you have the best of the past as well as the amenities of the present—lighted tennis courts, a swimming pool, conference facilities,
and airport shuttle service. The plantation also has a stocked fishing pond and a
jogging trail. Opulent Pebble Hill Plantation is open for tours nearby.

As you proceed south of Thomasville on US 319, turn right on Meridian
Road. The inn is several miles ahead on the right. Be alert: signage is inadequate
or nonexistent.

Myon Bed & Breakfast

Regina Wells, Innkeeper
Harold Harper, Owner
128 First Street
Tifton, GA 31793
912-382-0959

$40–$60 • Open all year • 3 rooms/suites •
B&B inn • Kids, no pets, smoking, provision
for disabled • Rating: 3

A treasure in Tifton was always the Old Myon Hotel. Long closed, it has been renovated and reopened for mixed use.

The street level contains City Hall, a restaurant, and several shops. Upstairs are two levels of office space and B&B rooms. To check in, take the elevator to the second floor and go to room 224. The guest rooms are all suites and are especially popular with business travelers or those staying for a long period. Family rates are available. Furnishings are simple antiques and collectibles. One unit has a full kitchen and two double beds. The two-bedroom suite has two baths and a balcony overlooking the other historic buildings of downtown Tifton, all of which is listed on the National Register of Historic Places.

A Continental breakfast of cereal, milk, juice, and a sweet roll is provided. The independently operated restaurant, which opens onto an airy courtyard, serves lunch daily except Saturday. It also has a private dining room that could be used for conferences or private parties.

From I-75, take the Second Street exit (exit 19). Go east to Love Avenue, then turn right onto First Street. The hotel is the largest building in the vicinity.

NEWLY OPENED

Country Inn
Sarah Jones
Route 2, Box 46A
Colquit, GA 31737
912-758-5417 or 800-453-6581

White House Bed & Breakfast
John and Mary Patterson
320 South Washington Street
Bainbridge, GA 31717-3982
912-248-1703

9

Presidential Pathways

This region was called home by two former presidents—Franklin Delano Roosevelt and Jimmy Carter. The region contains remnants of the antebellum and Civil War years as well as two major rivers, five reservoirs, rolling green hills, extensive pine forests, sight-seeing, bass fishing, whitewater rafting, camping, and cultural events—enough variety to please almost any visitor.

The best way to see the area is to follow the **Andersonville Trail**, a seventy-five-mile route off I-75. Exit the interstate onto State 127 at Perry. The trail meanders to **Marshallville**, home of the **National Headquarters of the American Camellia Society**, which maintains gardens, a greenhouse, a research library, and a collection of famous Boehm porcelain birds.

The highlight of the Andersonville Trail is the **Andersonville National Historic Site**—the infamous Civil War prison park and **National Cemetery**, the only national memorial for all prisoners of war.

The visitors center houses a museum, and wayside exhibits recreate the conditions that existed. Sometimes costumed guides demonstrate methods of controlling the captives. Camp Sumter, as it was officially known, was the largest Confederate military prison. More than 45,000 Union soldiers were confined here, of which 13,000 died from disease, malnutrition, overcrowding, and/or exposure. The prison ceased to exist when the war ended in May 1865.

The **Civil War Village of Andersonville** is a tiny, sleepy hamlet where prisoners arrived by rail and were marched the one-quarter mile to the fort. Nearby is a pioneer farm park with a log cabin, barn, farm animals, a sugarcane mill, and syrup kettle.

Tour nearby historic **Trebor Plantation**, established in 1833. The main house is Greek Revival style with Edwardian adaptations. Original hand-planed boards remain on the front facade and in two parlors. The grounds are dotted with traditional plantation dependencies (outbuildings) in the process of being restored.

Americus has a large historic district of antebellum and Victorian buildings. Walking and driving tours are available. **Pecan World**, one of the town's primary businesses, offers the delicious nuts in every form imaginable.

In **Plains**, visitors can take a self-guided tour. The **Depot Museum** houses pictures of Jimmy Carter and memorabilia from his boyhood through his presidency.

You'll find the southern end of the Andersonville Trail in **Cordele**. The downtown—included on the National Register of Historic Places—served as the state capital during the last days of the Confederacy. At nearby 8,500-acre **Lake Black-shear** you'll find the **Veterans Memorial State Park**.

Detouring west, explore **Lumpkin, Westville,** and **Providence Canyon.** In Lumpkin, visit the **Bedingfield Inn,** a restored 1836 stagecoach inn, the **Hatchett Drug Store Museum,** and the **Singer Hardware Store**—a genuine old-fashioned general store.

Nearby **Westville** is a functioning living history village in the tradition of Williamsburg, although not on such a grand scale. By restoring and relocating original buildings, a village has been created that realistically depicts Georgia's preindustrial life and the culture of the 1850s. Costumed guides dispense history, and craftsmen demonstrate their expertise.

Known as Georgia's "Little Grand Canyon," **Providence Canyon State Conservation Park** comes as a complete surprise to the first-time visitor. The result of erosion, the varicolored ravine walls produce a beautiful natural painting. In addition to spectacular panoramas, the park has the highest concentration of wildflowers in the state as well as a large number of plumleaf azaleas—found only in the Presidential Pathways region. The park includes an interpretive center, picnic areas, hiking and backpacking trails, pioneer camps, and a group shelter.

Columbus boasts the **Columbus Museum,** the **Confederate Naval Museum, Heritage Corner** of historic homes, and the **Springer Opera House**.

Fort Benning is the home of the **National Infantry Museum,** which traces the evolution of the infantry from the French and Indian War to the present.

In **LaGrange** visit the **Chattahoochee Valley Art Association,** located in the renovated 1892 Troup County Jail. **Bellevue** is an 1852 Greek Revival home built by statesman Benjamin Harvey Hill. On the campus of LaGrange College—Georgia's oldest independent school—is the **Lamar Dodd Art Center,** which features changing exhibits, a permanent collection, and retrospective works by Dodd as well as the Southwest and Plains American Indian collection.

Nearby 25,900-acre **West Point Lake** boasts some of the best fishing in Georgia. Recreational facilities include two commercial marinas, four beaches, six major camping areas, and a 10,000-acre wildlife management area.

In **Newnan,** visit the **Male Academy Museum,** which interprets Coweta County's history from its Indian heritage through the 1900s. Newnan has a significant district of historic homes, several of which are open for tours. The town is also known for its antique shops. Arrange with the Chamber of Commerce to tour **Windmere Plantation**.

Oglethorpe, a Mennonite community, is also the home of **Whitewater Creek Park,** a 500-acre preserve. **Florence Marina State Park** is at Omaha on the shores of **Lake Walter F. George**.

Buena Vista, billed as "America's front porch," is going to give Nashville and Branson some competition. Already open for business are an **Elvis Collection Museum**, the **National Country Music Museum**, the **Silver Moon Music Barn**, and the **Front Porch Music Hall**. Nearby is **Pasaquan**, the folk art compound of the late Edward Owens Martin—sometimes known as Saint EOM.

Thomaston has walking or driving tours of the historic district. The **Flint Outdoor Center** provides canoeing, rafting, and shooting class I, II, and III rapids for the adventurous. Visit the **Achumpkee Covered Bridge**, one of the few remaining in the state.

Roosevelt's **Little White House** in **Warm Springs** features original furnishings, personal memorabilia, his hand-controlled Ford, and a famous unfinished portrait. Also on the grounds is a museum that contains other keepsakes from his presidency.

The town of **Warm Springs** has been restored to its 1940s appearance. It features sixty-five shops, seven restaurants, and many festivals and special events throughout the year.

One of Georgia's most renowned attractions is **Callaway Gardens**. The 2,500-acre resort boasts 700 varieties of azaleas—including the rare plumleaf—as well as the world's largest display of holly. The garden's **Day Butterfly Center** is an immense glass-enclosed conservatory. The **John A. Sibley Horticultural Center** offers five acres of floral displays that change with the season as well as a two-story indoor/outdoor waterfall. Other attractions at the resort include golf courses, thirteen lakes, walking and driving trails, a beach, annual golf tournaments, and the November Steeplechase.

The Cottage Inn
Jim and Billie Gatewood
State Highway 49
Americus, GA 31709
912-924-9316 or 912-924-8995

$55–$60 • Open all year • 1 room, 2 suites
• Home stay/guest cottage • Ask about kids
no pets, restricted smoking, reservations
required, no credit cards • Rating: 4

The Cottage Inn is one of the most beautiful B&Bs we've seen—both the accommodations and the setting. The two antebellum-style guest cottages sit well back from the highway amidst manicured lawns.

Guest rooms have high ceilings, decorative fireplaces, modern baths, ceiling fans, and phones. They are exquisitely furnished with fine antiques, Oriental rugs, old quilts, blue and white porcelains, and flower arrangements. Twelve-foot floor-to-ceiling windows overlook the grounds, including a private veranda where you can rock while you watch the peacocks strut by. The property boasts a swimming pool and a clay tennis court, which guests are encouraged to use.

A Continental breakfast of cereals, fruit, Danish pastry, juice, and hot beverage is served. A full breakfast can be provided with prior notice.

From US 280 north, take State 49 to Americus. The inn is one mile ahead on the right.

Guerry House, 1833/
Springhill Plantation

Pamela and Walter Stapleton
723 McGarrah Street
Americus, GA 31709
912-924-1009

$55-$85 • Open all year • 5 rooms • B&B inn
• Kids, no pets, no smoking • Rating: 4

An unusual style for Southwest Georgia, the Guerry House is an example of Louisiana raised-cottage construction. Built entirely by slaves, it was begun in 1833 and finished in 1836 for Rep. James P. Guerry. The two-story house is assembled from hand-hewn yellow pine with pegged mortise and tendon construction. A veranda with front and back staircases completely encircles the house. Other architectural features of note include handblown glass, six fireplaces, and a cypress shingled roof. Restoration took ten years. The owners now live in the lower level, where they maintain a Confederate library and an extensive collection of related artifacts. Recording artists, the Stapletons are also active in Civil War reenactments.

Guest rooms, which have private baths, are in two historic outbuildings that have been moved from other locations in Georgia. Furnishings are primitive heart-pine furniture and other antiques. Custom-made wrought-iron details enhance the decor. The Honeymoon Suite features a Jacuzzi.

A full southern breakfast is served in the country kitchen. The Stapletons provide gourmet dining for luncheons and dinners by reservation only.

The landscaped grounds and gardens, which overlook a small pond, feature the original carriage house and well. Stroll the twenty-six acres where Civil War reenactments are held periodically.

McGarrah Street branches east off US 19. North of downtown, the B&B is the first house on the left.

The Morris Manor

Troy and Betsy Morris
425 Timberlane Drive
Americus, GA 31709
912-924-4884

$45-$75 • Open all year • 5 rooms • Home
stay • Kids over 12, no pets, no smoking,
reservations required, no credit cards • Rating: 3

This Georgian colonial-style home of recent construction is located in a heavily wooded subdivision amid pecan and fruit trees.

Guest rooms are named after the children in the Morris family, most of whom are grown and gone. The furnishings in each room are a mixture of styles. Three rooms have private baths; two share a bath. Family rates are available. Morris Manor is particularly popular with business travelers.

Coffee is served in the upstairs hall in the morning. Then guests settle in the large country kitchen or dining room for their breakfast, which may include juice, coffee cake, muffins, biscuits, an omelette or a casserole, pancakes, or waffles. In season, you'll be treated to fresh fruit from the Morris's orchard.

Children can enjoy the trampoline and other play equipment. Everyone can relax with a walk through the orchard of fruit and pecan trees behind the house, or on a walking tour of the town's large historic district.

From downtown Americus, go east on Lamar through town until the street becomes State 27 toward Vienna. Go one-quarter mile until you see a white brick church on the right. Turn right onto Dellwood, then left onto Ashley. Go two blocks to the top of the hill, where the street dead-ends into Timberlane. The inn is directly ahead of you.

A Place Away Cottage

Peggy and Fred Sheppard
110 Oglethorpe Street
Andersonville, GA 31711
912-924-1044 or 912-924-2558

$40-$50 • Open all year • 2 rooms • Home
stay/guest house • Kids, no pets, smoking,
no credit cards • Rating: 3½

Peggy Sheppard says it best: "The rates are old-fashioned, the beds are comfortable, the breakfast hearty, and the hospitality southern." Once a sharecropper's cottage, this small, rustic, turn-of-the-century house has been converted to a B&B.

The cottage features a tin roof, heart-pine ceilings, stenciled floors, and ceiling fans—although it is air conditioned. The two guest rooms share a small common room with a pay phone—supplied with quarters—and a microwave. The common room is between the guest rooms, which permits two separate couples to stay with privacy, but can be opened up for a family.

Each room has a private bath, fireplace, cable TV, coffeemaker, and refrigerator. Rooms are decorated in simple country antiques. A gift of fruit will be waiting for you. Rates are $40 single and $50 double, but are discounted $5 if you do not want breakfast.

Check-in is at the Sheppard's house across the street. Because the house is large (it was once the town school), you may have to ring the doorbell repeatedly to get the innkeepers' attention.

A Continental breakfast is placed in the common room. You may choose to eat it there, in your room, on the porch, or at a picnic table in the yard. A hobo poke is provided so you can carry along any treats not eaten for breakfast. The cottage has a barbecue grill and picnic table for guests' use.

The front porch rockers provide a fine place to relax at the end of the day. The town tennis court is next door, and guests can also play chip golf nearby. The inn is only one and a half blocks from the historic Andersonville Civil War Village, pioneer farm, and walking tour.

From I-75 south of Macon, exit onto State 49 toward Andersonville. Turn right on State 271. Turn right at Oglethorpe, the first major cross street. The cottage is on the right, but check-in is on the left.

Lora's Bed & Breakfast

Chris Rogers
229 Broad Street
Buena Vista, GA 31803
912-649-7307 or 800-836-Y'ALL (9255)

$40–$50 • Open all year • 3 rooms • B&B inn
• Kids, no pets, no smoking • Rating: 3½

Young, energetic Chris Rogers runs a trio of B&Bs in Buena Vista—Yesteryear Inn, McGraw House, and Lora's. Named for former Buena Vista teacher Miss Lora Mathis, this small Victorian house was built between 1875 and 1880. The three guest rooms are decorated primarily with English antiques and have private baths and queen-size beds with picket-fence headboards.

Choose from the Green Room; the Red, White, and Blue Room; or the largest and nicest—Miss Lora's Room. Her room features a huge bathroom with a tub and shower, a dressing room, and big closets. Family rates are available.

Guests at Lora's can choose to eat their breakfast there or at the Yesteryear Inn. The generous country breakfast might include fruit pizza, country ham, cheese grits, croissants, and baked French toast stuffed with cream cheese.

Guests can relax in the cozy tongue-and-groove-paneled den, which has a Franklin stove, TV, and telephone. Other lounging spots include the wraparound front porch and the private backyard.

You'll probably check in at the Yesteryear Inn at 229 Broad Street, which is also State 41. The Yesteryear is three-quarters of a mile south of the courthouse square. Lora's is actually on Third Avenue.

McGraw House

Chris Rogers
229 Broad Street
Buena Vista, GA 31803
912-649-7307 or 800-836-Y'ALL (9255)

$40-$60 • Open all year • 4 rooms • B&B inn
• Kids, no pets, no smoking • Rating: 3½

Chris Rogers is the energetic innkeeper of a trio of B&Bs in Buena Vista—Yesteryear Inn, Lora's, and McGraw House. Built in 1900, McGraw House sits amidst a broad lawn in a quiet residential neighborhood. It is furnished in period antiques.

Guest rooms have private baths. The Front Room is adorned by a decorative fireplace and has a queen-size bed and a private screened-in porch. Both the Mauve Room and the Blue Room have double beds. Unique to the Blue Room are a picket-fence headboard and window treatments embellished with neckties.

Guests at the McGraw House may choose to have breakfast there or at Yesteryear Inn. The generous country breakfast might include fruit pizza, country ham, cheese grits, croissants, and baked French toast stuffed with cream cheese.

Guests can lounge in the formal living room or in the backyard. Family rates are available.

You'll probably check in at the Yesteryear Inn at 229 Broad Street, which is also State 41. The Yesteryear is three-quarters of a mile south of the courthouse square. McGraw House is actually at 130 Second Avenue.

Morgan Towne House

Claudine and Richard Morgan
2 Church Street
Buena Vista, GA 31803
912-649-3663

$50–$60 • Open almost all year • 3 rooms
• Country inn • Kids, no pets, restricted
smoking, reservations required • Rating: 4

The Morgan Towne House offers lodging and dining in a restored 1880 Victorian mansion. The Morgan's motto is, "We serve Sunday dinner every day."

As with most Victorians, this one is encased by a wraparound porch filled with rockers. Step into the towering foyer and admire the ornate woodwork and columns. All the downstairs rooms, complete with decorative fireplaces, are utilized for restaurant seating.

An original stained-glass window adorns the stairway. The three spacious upstairs bedrooms are decorated in antiques and reproductions and have huge private bathrooms with claw-foot tubs. Guest rooms have a TV with VCR. (There's a video store just across the street for easy rentals.) Two rooms are equipped with an extra daybed.

A full country breakfast of your choice can be served in the dining room, on the porch, or in your room.

The inn is closed May 31 through June 4 and December 24 through 31. Otherwise, the restaurant is open for a buffet lunch Tuesday through Sunday. Dinner is served Friday and Saturday. The facility and catering are available for weddings, receptions, and parties; decorated cakes can be provided if arrangements are made ahead. The Morgans can organize a hunt for deer, quail, or turkey in season.

Church Street is one block east of the courthouse square. The Morgan Towne House is between Fourth Avenue and State 26.

Yesteryear Inn

Chris Rogers
229 Broad Street
Buena Vista, GA 31803
912-649-7307 or 800-836-Y'ALL (9255)

$40–$50 • Open all year • 4 rooms • Home stay
• Kids, no pets, restricted smoking • Rating: 3½

Yesteryear occupies an 1866 farmhouse located in a pecan grove three-quarters of a mile south of Buena Vista's courthouse square. The innkeeper, Chris Rogers, also operates Lora's and McGraw House in Buena Vista.

Originally owned by the town doctor, Yesteryear was passed to his oldest daughter and her husband. Although they eventually sold the house, it remained in the next family from 1915 to 1987. Chris was fortunate enough to buy the house completely furnished, including the china, crystal, love letters, thirteen trunks, fifteen quilts, and the biggest dogwood in Georgia. It is more than eighty years old. Chris did a professional job of refurbishing the house and adding the guest bathrooms himself.

Typical of the period in which the house was built, there are four rooms downstairs and four rooms upstairs, with heart-pine floors throughout.

The downstairs guest room is called the Doctor's Room and is filled with pre-1930s medical memorabilia. The room has a private bath and a feather bed. The three upstairs bedrooms share a bath. Several rooms have decorative fireplaces.

Other lovely features of the house are the two vast porches—one downstairs, one upstairs—supported by large white columns.

The B&B is particularly popular with business travelers and military personnel. Family rates are available.

A generous country breakfast of fruit pizza, country ham, cheese grits, croissants, and baked French toast stuffed with cream cheese is served in the dining room. Chris serves evening desserts with coffee on the upstairs porch in good weather or in the parlor.

Broad Street is also State 41. The inn is three-quarters of a mile south of the courthouse square.

Inn Scarlett's Footsteps

K. C. and Vern Bassham
138 Hill Street
Concord, GA 30206
800-886-7355

$55–$65 • Open all year • 5 rooms • B&B inn
• No kids, no pets, no smoking • Rating: 4½

This may be as close to Tara as you'll ever get. This stunning brick antebellum-style mansion, with a circular drive sweeping through magnolia-dotted grounds to the soaring-columned front porch, is surrounded by acres of horse farm. K. C. says of the inn, "We're living our dream. . . . We sell fantasy."

The house, built in 1905, has inlaid hardwood floors, twelve-foot ceilings, and original chandeliers and ceiling medallions. Rooms are furnished in antiques and period reproductions. The inn also serves as a museum for K. C.'s extensive collection of *Gone With the Wind* memorabilia. The mansion and museum are open for tours Tuesday through Sunday afternoons.

Guest rooms are named for *Gone With the Wind* characters. Scarlett's Room has a life-size mannequin dressed in an alluring ball gown. Melanie's Room is light and airy and filled with wicker and delicate floral fabrics. Each guest room has a private bath and decorative fireplace.

A full breakfast is served on the informal screened porch in good weather, or in the massive formal dining room.

In addition to serving as a catering facility for weddings, receptions, luncheons, and company parties, the inn holds twelve Barbecue and Ball events annually. Participants are encouraged to come dressed as their favorite *Gone With the Wind* character.

Take US 19 south from Atlanta to Zebulon, then turn right onto State 18. Follow it to Concord. The inn is 0.4 mile on the right.

Fern Brook Inn Bed & Breakfast

Margie and Harmon Head
101 Wilson Street
Ellaville, GA 31806
912-937-5672

$40-$47 • Open all year • 2 suites • Home
stay • No kids, no pets, restricted smoking
• Rating: 3

One wing of this graceful Victorian cottage—located downtown on the main street—has been converted to two completely private suites.

One suite has a bedroom and a separate sitting room. This suite sleeps four—two in the bedroom and two on the bed in the sitting room. The second suite is one large room with a sofa, a sitting area, an electric fireplace, a work area with desk and phone, and a brass bed. This suite sleeps two. Both suites have a private bath and a partial kitchen with a refrigerator/freezer, sink, cabinets, coffee-maker, and counter with two stools. Despite the lack of an oven or microwave, the suite is ideal for a business traveler or someone making a long stay.

A Continental-plus breakfast is left in the kitchen of each suite for guests to enjoy at their leisure. Breakfast includes cereal, muffins, juice, and fruit. Fixings are available for making hot beverages. Always handy are juice, soft drinks, fruit, treats, crackers, and bottled water. Evening turn-down service includes a mint on your pillow.

Fern Brook Inn is just off US 19 in the center of Ellaville. Turn east at the courthouse corner. Pass one block of commercial buildings, and the B&B is straight in front of you in the Y in the road. During the day, check in with Margie at her store, The Emporium.

Annie's Log Cabin

Bobbie West
(located in Hamilton, GA)
Mailing address:
305 West 5th Street
Donalsonville, GA 31745
706-628-5729

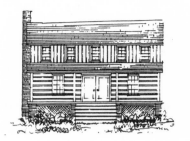

$75–$95 • Open all year • 1 cabin • Home
stay/guest house • Kids over 6, no pets,
smoking, no credit cards • Rating: 3

For those who want to get away from it all, this historic 1854 modified dogtrot log cabin is completely isolated on twenty acres. The house backs up to deep woods with hiking trails and a stream. However, you get the feel of isolation without the inconvenience because the cabin isn't far out of town.

No one lives on the property full-time, so the gate is locked across the dirt access road. You probably couldn't find it by yourself anyway, so you call from town and a hostess escorts you to the property and gets you settled in.

As you would expect with a log cabin, the furnishings are rustic and casual and the atmosphere is informal. There's a big porch across the front with comfortable rockers. The cozy great room has a fireplace, TV, phone, ceiling fan, books, games, and magazines. The two guest rooms sleep eight—one downstairs bedroom has two doubles and the loft has two doubles. Guests share the bath and the full kitchen with three tables. There is a washer and dryer, air-conditioning downstairs, and an attic fan and window air conditioner upstairs. The house is ideal for a family, a group of friends, or a small corporate meeting. The rate is for two people; each additional person is $10 extra. A senior citizen rate of $65 is available for those over age fifty-five.

Your hostess will leave the fixings for you to create your own breakfast of cereal, milk, juice, breads, cinnamon rolls, and hot beverages.

Hamilton is at the junction of US 27 and State 116. From Hamilton, call Bobbie to meet you, guide you to the property, and unlock the gate.

Wedgwood Bed & Breakfast

Janice Neuffer
US 27
Hamilton, GA 31811
706-628-5659

$58-$73 • Open all year • 3 rooms • Home stay
• Kids, no pets, no smoking, no credit cards
• Rating: 3

Blue accents with designs stenciled in white and a large collection of the famous blue and white Wedgwood ceramics earn this restored mid-1800s Greek Revival home its name.

The house sits in the middle of town along a major highway. However, once you've entered the house or the backyard, the modern world slips away.

Exceptionally beautiful decorative brackets support the front porch balcony. Inside, the twenty-two-inch-wide wall planking shows the marks of hand planing. Period antiques and memorabilia mixed with modern furnishings give the house a feeling of warmth and comfort. Downstairs rooms—including a formal parlor, library, and den—are for guests' use. The upstairs hall can also double as a guest sitting room. Guest rooms all have private baths. Fresh flowers and/or fruit will be waiting in you room. Honeymooners are pampered with nightly turn-down service. Family rates are available.

Janice serves an outstanding full breakfast in the dining room using her china, crystal, and silver. This breakfast might include German pancakes with a side dish of fruit, French toast, homemade breads, meat, hot preserves, a fruit quiche, cereal, juice, and hot beverages. If you prefer to sleep in, you can request a Continental breakfast the night before.

Guests are invited to use the piano, and the TV and VCR in the cozy den. Janice has a wonderful collection of classic films.

The porches and backyard are major attractions at this B&B. One porch is well supplied with rockers and also features a swing, picnic table, ceiling fan, and lots of hanging ferns. The fenced backyard has a gazebo with a hammock as well as a huge magnolia and a small formal garden. Five stalls in the carport provide covered parking.

The inn is in the center of Hamilton, on the corner of US 27 and Mobley.

The Fair Oaks Inn
Ken Hammock
703 East Main Street
Hogansville, GA 30230
706-637-8828

$50–$75 • Open all year • 2 rooms, 2 suites
• B&B inn • Kids over 14, no pets, restricted
smoking • Rating: 4½

The Fair Oaks Inn is a striking turn-of-the-century Victorian Queen Anne home on the site of the original 1835 plantation. The gaily painted yellow mansion sits well back from the street behind formal Victorian gardens and manicured lawns. The house is reached by a brick driveway ending in a heart-shaped turnaround. The front is embellished with a wraparound porch filled with swings and rockers.

Restored to its original elegance, the mansion is furnished with exquisite antiques. It has pocket doors, original fretwork and stained glass, nine working fireplaces, and striking window treatments. The public rooms include a formal sitting room, formal dining room, and library and upstairs sitting room with a TV, VCR, and a large library of movies.

Guest rooms and suites have gas fireplaces and double, king-, or queen-size beds. The downstairs guest room has a private bath down the hall. The upstairs guest room shares a bath with the innkeeper. The Master Suite has a canopy bed, two fireplaces, a sitting room, and a bath with a large Jacuzzi and separate steam shower. The Carriage House has a bedroom, sitting room, bath, and dressing room. The inn is particularly appropriate for business travelers or small corporate meetings.

Behind the house is a spectacular English garden that includes small ponds with fountains, a large swimming pool, a gazebo, several lattice-covered swings, and several converted gas street lamps from New Orleans.

A full gourmet breakfast is served in the formal dining room or on the sunporch. Complimentary wine and cheese are served in the afternoon in the library or, weather permitting, in the garden.

From I-85, take exit 6 onto State 54/100. Go west about 2.7 miles. Just past a small historic cemetery on the left, look for the discreet sign for Fair Oaks.

Limberlost: The Evers' House

John and Sharon Evers
130 LaGrange Street
Newnan, GA 30263
404-254-8145

$50–$70 • Open all year • 1 room or suite
• Home stay • No kids, no pets, restricted
smoking, reservations required, no credit cards
• Rating: 4

Limberlost is a restored 1860s Victorian house listed on the National Register of Historic Places. It was named after the book *Girl of Limberlost*.

Guests may use either the guest room alone or the room combined with a parlor to create a suite. Accommodations overlook the white-columned porch as well as the expansive backyard beyond with its gardens and pool.

The house is appropriately furnished in simple period antiques. The guest room has a private entrance, private bath, and such extras as a bed tray and back-rest. The sitting room has comfortable seating around a decorative fireplace. The well-tended two-and-a-half-acre lot boasts a swimming pool, a grape arbor, and a hammock that invites you to while away the day. A tiny shop in the sitting room sells crafts and Georgia items. Corporate rates are available.

A Continental breakfast is served in your room, or on the large wraparound porch in good weather. You'll be offered a glass of wine upon arrival.

From I-85, take exit 9 and go west on State 34, which is also Jefferson Street. Turn right onto Bullsboro, then left onto Jackson, which becomes LaGrange. The house is on the left.

Parrott-Camp-Soucy Home
Richard Cousins and Martha Sosa
155 Greenville Street
Newnan, GA 30263
404-502-0676

$90–$110 • Open almost all year • 4 rooms
• Home stay • Ask about kids, no pets, no
smoking, reservations required • Rating: 4½

Winner of many state and national preservation awards, including one from the National Trust for Historic Preservation and another from the Georgia Trust for Historic Preservation, this gorgeous 1886 Second Empire Victorian mansion is a magnificent example of the period. As well as appearing in countless magazine articles, this B&B is showcased in the book *Daughters of the Painted Ladies*.

The mansion is located on a two-acre lot in a historic neighborhood where most of the homes have been lovingly restored. Newnan offers walking or driving tours that include this area.

Twelve-foot ceilings, burnished woods, intricate moldings, and exquisite Victorian antiques grace the elegant interior. Guest rooms are decorated in antiques and feature decorative fireplaces. All four rooms have a private bath with claw-foot tubs with showers and reproduction water closets. The B&B also features a Jacuzzi. Guests are invited to use the downstairs parlor, the upstairs sitting room, and the third-floor billiard room with its antique billiard table built in 1851.

Well-tended lawns and a Victorian garden surrounding the mansion can be viewed from the wicker-filled wraparound porch. The backyard boasts a fish pond, swimming pool, comfortable lawn furniture, a shady gazebo, and a hammock.

A full breakfast is served in the dining room or breakfast room. Wine and beer are available for guests.

From I-85, take exit 9 and go west on State 34, which becomes Jefferson and then Greenville. The inn is on the right four blocks from the courthouse.

The Storms House
Jan and Dallas Storms
Harris Street
Pine Mountain, GA 31822
706-663-9100

$95-$130 • Open all year • 4 rooms, 1 cottage
• Home stay • Ask about kids, no pets, no
smoking, provision for disabled, no credit cards
• Rating: 4

Built in the 1890s, this 7,000-square-foot imposing Victorian in the heart of Pine Mountain features twelve-foot ceilings, hardwood floors, claw-foot tubs, ornate moldings, and decorative fireplaces. Although the rooms are painted in dark, bold colors, the many large windows keep the interior light and airy. Guests are encouraged to enjoy the downstairs sitting rooms, the massive wraparound porch amply furnished with rockers and old-fashioned swings, and the small upstairs porch with a swing. Jan's exquisite doll collection is on display throughout the house.

All guest rooms have decorative fireplaces and private baths with a claw-foot or pedestal tub. The downstairs King George Room has an antique bedroom suite original to the house, and a ramp, separate entrance, and bathroom modifications to make the accommodations handicapped accessible.

Upstairs, the Queen Victoria Room has a brass double bed, a daybed in a large bay window, and a private bath down the hall. The Prince Charles Room has a queen-size bed. The Queen Anne Room, the largest, has a painted floor stenciled with ivy, two iron double beds, wicker rockers, a ceiling fan, and a huge bath with a pedestal tub, separate shower, and large vanity.

Simpson Cottage, decorated in equestrian motif, has a great room with TV, kitchen facilities, two bedrooms, and a bath—making it ideal for a family or a party wanting a long-term stay. Cottage guests are welcome to use the brick patio and gas grill.

A full breakfast is served in the formal dining room. Breakfast is not included for guests of the cottage.

Coming into town on US 27 south from Atlanta, Harris is the first right turn after the block of historic buildings.

The Plains Bed
and Breakfast Inn

Grace Jackson
100 West Church Street
Plains, GA 31780
912-824-7252

$50 • Open all year • 4 rooms • Home stay
• Kids, ask about pets, smoking, credit cards
discouraged • Rating: 3

Whoever heard of Plains before Jimmy Carter became president? Now who hasn't heard of it? Plains is a turn-of-the-century railroad and agricultural town filled with historic Victorian homes.

One of these attractive homes is now the Plains Bed and Breakfast Inn. Painted a soft rose pink, the house overlooks the town center, a park, and the Carter Welcome Center. The structure was once a boardinghouse where Miss Lillian—Carter's mother—lived in her single and early married days until just before Carter was born. She and her husband moved because the doctor didn't want her climbing the stairs.

Watch the unhurried world go by from the porch swing or the wicker rockers on the front porch. Inside the foyer, you can't help but admire the two gorgeously carved staircases and the intricate ceilings. Guests are invited to use the downstairs parlor and TV. Upstairs are the guest rooms, a wicker-filled parlor, and a substantial library.

Guest rooms all are furnished with antiques and have private baths, decorative fireplaces, and queen-size beds. The Front Room has its own upstairs porch.

Business travelers like the pampering they get at this B&B. Corporate and long-term rates are available.

A full breakfast of grits, eggs, sausage, a selection of breads, and homemade jellies is served in the formal dining room.

When you arrive in town via US 280 from Americus, the B&B is on the right, across from the police department.

The Veranda
Bobby and Jan Boal
252 Seavy Street
Senoia, GA 30276-0177
404-599-3905

$65-$105 • Open all year • 9 rooms • Country
inn • Ask about kids, no pets, smoking
restricted, provision for disabled • Rating: 4½

Built in 1906 as the Hollberg Hotel, this structure has been restored and returned
to its original use. Today the romantic Victorian is listed on the National Register
of Historic Places and was named the 1990-91 Inn of the Year by *B&Bs, Inns and
Guest Houses in the U.S. and Canada*. Ably run by energetic Bobby and Jan Boal,
the inn features a restaurant and a gift shop.

The neoclassical structure has a sweeping wraparound porch accented with
classical Doric columns. Inside are two parlors—one a music room with a working
1860 Estey reed organ and a Wurlitzer player piano complete with numerous music
rolls, organ, and chimes. A crystal chandelier hangs from the tin ceiling in the
cavernous central hall.

Guest rooms are furnished with antiques. Some rooms feature queen-size
beds and decorative fireplaces; all offer private baths. The Honeymoon Suite has a
bay window, a sofa, and a Jacuzzi. The three front bedrooms can be closed off to
create a suite. The inn has a ramp, two downstairs bedrooms, and modified
bathrooms to accommodate the physically impaired. The Veranda is suitable for
business travelers and small corporate retreats.

The upstairs hall serves as a well-stocked library and game room. Guests can
relax in the parlors, the library, in rockers and swings on the porch, or in the side
garden with stone seats and a small decorative pool with a fountain.

A full southern breakfast is offered in the dining room, which also serves
lunch and a five-course dinner by reservation as well as afternoon and evening
desserts. The dining room is popular for bridal luncheons, wedding receptions,
and other private parties.

Bobby has two unusual collections—kaleidoscopes and ornate canes. He'll
be more than happy to explain their unique histories or unusual features.

From State 85 south of Atlanta, turn west on Seavy. The inn is at the
corner of Seavy and Barnes. From State 16, turn north at Broad. The inn is at
the intersection with Seavy.

Whitfield Inn
Barbara Grace
327 West Main Street
Thomaston, GA 30286
706-647-2482

$45–$55 • Open all year • 5 rooms • Home stay
• Kids, pets, smoking • Rating: 3

Popular with business travelers because of its convenience to downtown, this graceful Victorian was built in 1883 as a one-story cottage. In 1907 a second story was added. The house sits well back from the street on an ample, shady lot. As is typical of Victorian construction, the house features a large wraparound porch.

The interior is tastefully furnished in antiques. A downstairs guest room has a private bath. Upstairs, two guest rooms have private baths. Two others that share a bath can be combined to create a suite. All rooms have a TV, phone, and radio. Several rooms are appointed with decorative fireplaces and ceiling fans. Guests are invited to use either of the sitting rooms or to enjoy the porches and yard. Rates are $45 single, and $55 double. A huge carport provides covered parking.

A full breakfast is served in the small dining room. It might consist of fruit, eggs, bacon, pecan waffles, and peaches and cream. Other meals can be provided on request with advance arrangements. Fresh fruit is always available for healthy munching.

The Flint River, within easy driving distance, offers swimming, fishing, and canoeing.

The B&B is located one and a half blocks off the courthouse square on US 19 on the south side of West Main.

Woodall House

Charlene and Bill Woodall
324 West Main Street
Thomaston, GA 30286
706-647-7044

$38–$46 • Open all year • 4 rooms • Home stay
• Kids, no pets, smoking, no credit cards
• Rating: 3

This attractive turn-of-the-century home is located close to downtown, making it especially appealing to business travelers.

One of the most alluring features of this house is the columned front porch amply supplied with wicker furniture and rockers. When weather permits, the porch is lush with flowers and hanging ferns.

Two guest rooms have a private bath with shower; the other two share a bath. All rooms have a decorative fireplace, TV, and ceiling fan. Family rates are available.

A Continental-plus or full breakfast is served in the dining room. Coffee, juice, and soft drinks are always available.

The Flint River, with swimming, canoeing, and fishing, is close by. As you approach the river, there are some spectacular views of how much erosion has taken place for the river to be located so far below the surrounding countryside.

The B&B is located one and a half blocks off the courthouse square on US 19 on the north side of West Main.

Hotel Warm Springs

Gerrie and Lee Thompson
17 Broad Street
Warm Springs, GA 31830
706-655-2114

$60–$160 • Open all year • 14 rooms, 2 suites
• Country inn • Kids, no pets, restricted
smoking • Rating: 5

Drive into the tiny crossroads that is Warm Springs and you'll be transported back to the 1940s. Imagine Franklin D. Roosevelt's chauffeur-driven convertible pulling up to the drugstore in the Hotel Warm Springs so the president could get a Coke and chat with the townsfolk. The three-story hotel has been restored to its 1941 appearance by its proud owners, Lee and Gerrie Thompson. In the tiny lobby, sixteen-foot ceilings loom over an ancient reception desk, as well as the original switchboard, typewriter, and telephone booth. Off the lobby, in what was once the drugstore, is a restaurant open for lunch and dinner. You'll also find an ice cream parlor—be sure to taste their homemade peach ice cream—and gift shops. The second floor mezzanine is a large, gracious sitting/dining area where guests are encouraged to congregate for a complimentary arrival cocktail as well as for the full country breakfast. A small, informal social parlor invites guests to watch TV, work on a gigantic jigsaw puzzle, or play checkers, cards, or other games as they mingle with fellow guests. In good weather, you can sit outside in the tiny garden with willow chairs and a swing.

The spacious, high-ceilinged guest rooms are filled with Roosevelt memorabilia, antiques, collectibles, and the simple furniture of the thirties and forties. Modern amenities include private baths, queen-size beds, and color TV. Some bathrooms have original claw-foot tubs and antique reproduction showers. The hotel is perfect for business travelers and corporate retreats. Inquire about corporate, group, and senior rates.

The Moncrief Room is furnished entirely with heirlooms from Gerrie's family—its prize is the 100-year-old iron bed. The Presidential Suite boasts a bedroom and parlor as well as original oak furniture made in Eleanor Roosevelt's Val-Kill shop. The Honeymoon Suite has a red heart-shaped Jacuzzi for two.

The hotel sits at the crossroads of US 27 and State 85 west as you enter town.

Index by Name

*We've stayed here.

Index by City